François-Marie Banier

NEVER STOP DANCING

STEIDL

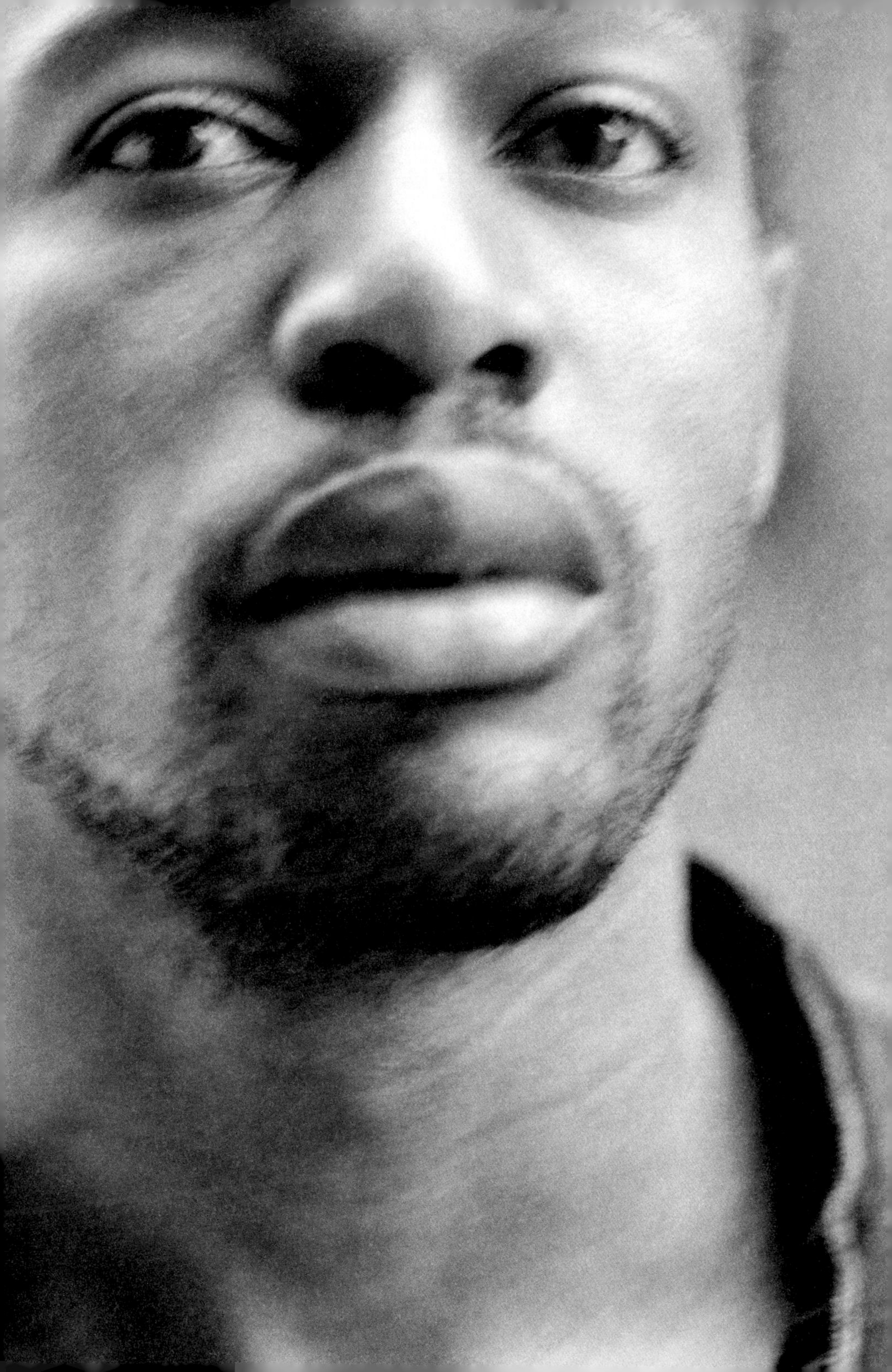

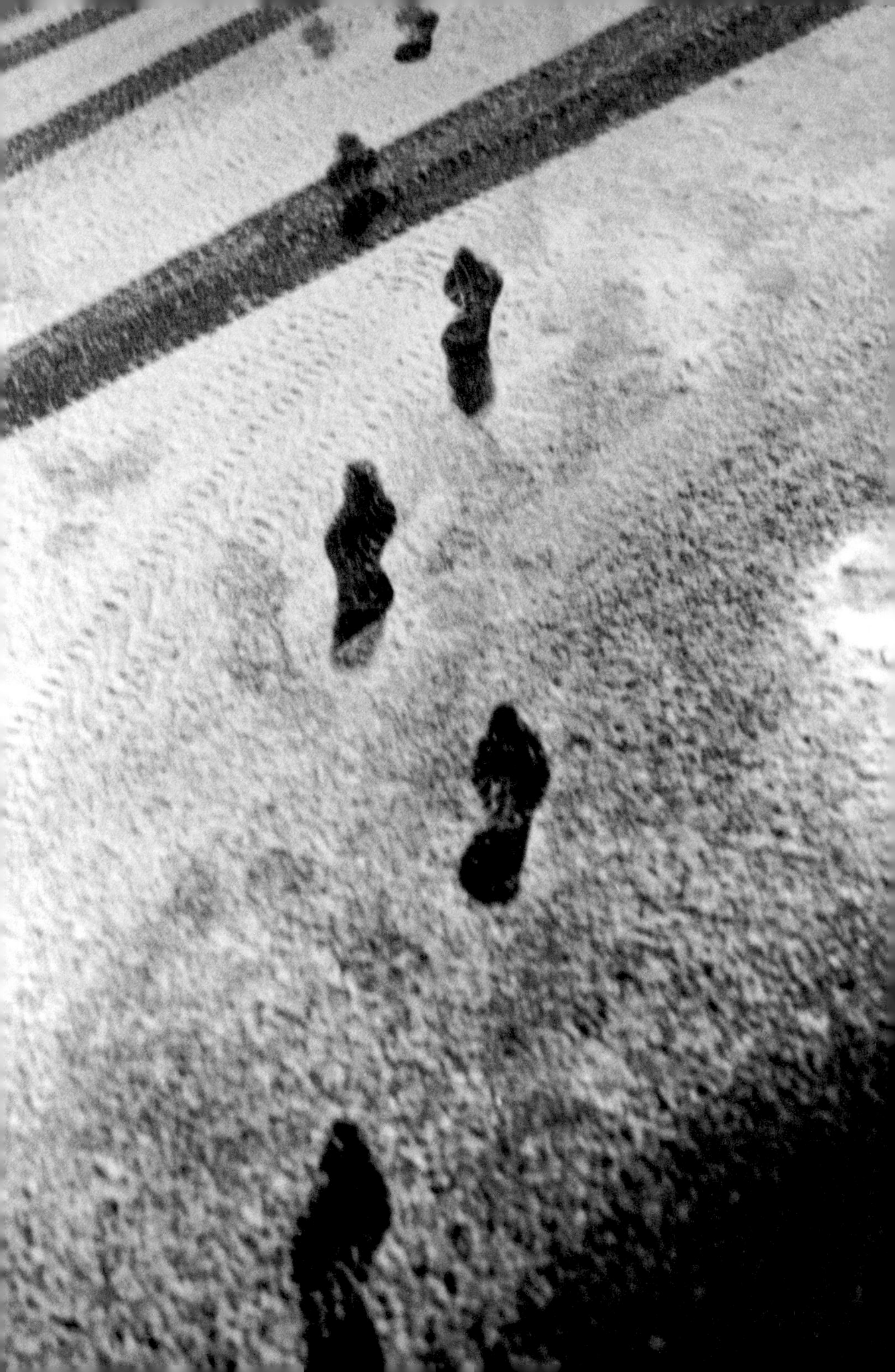

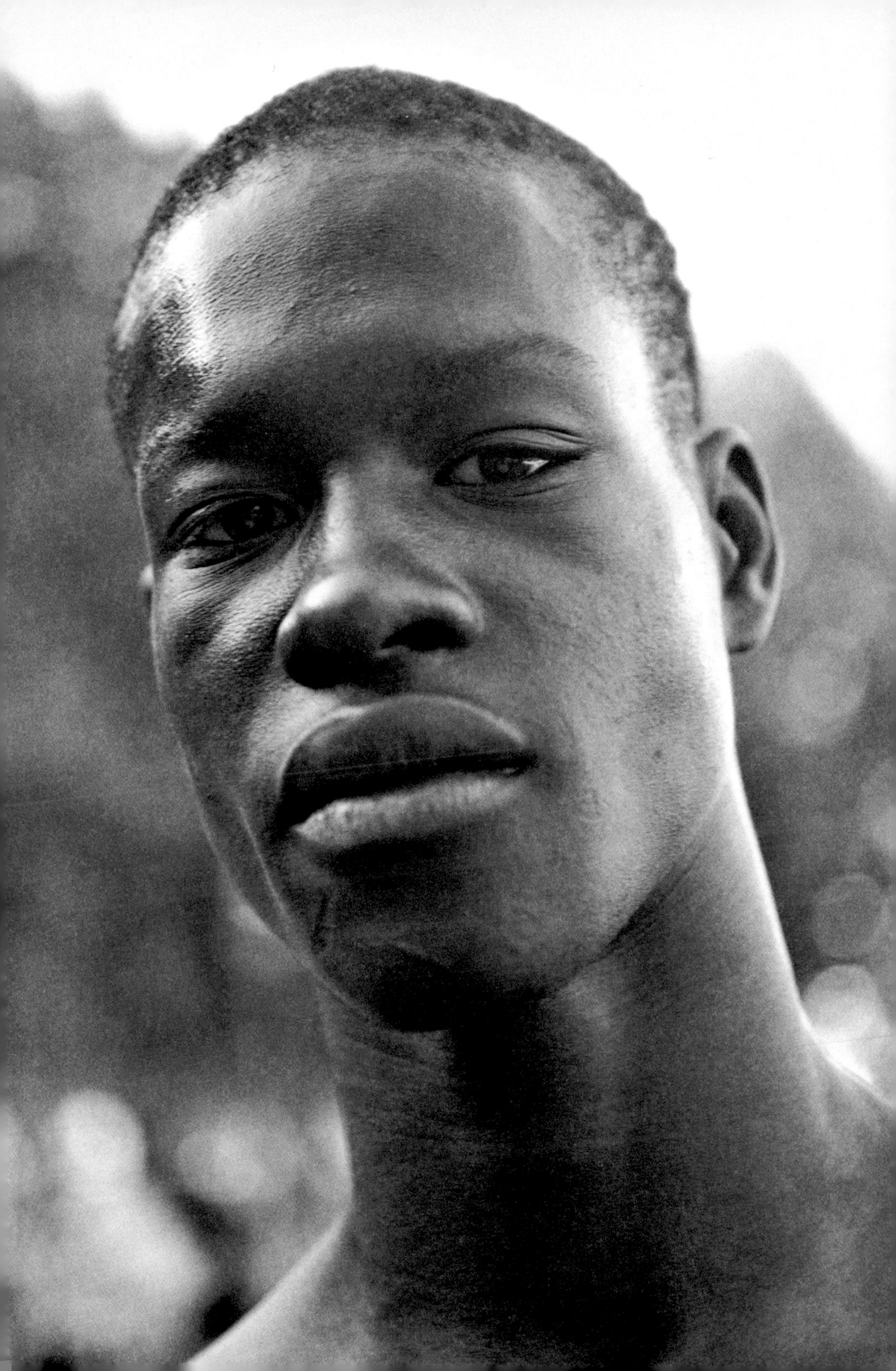

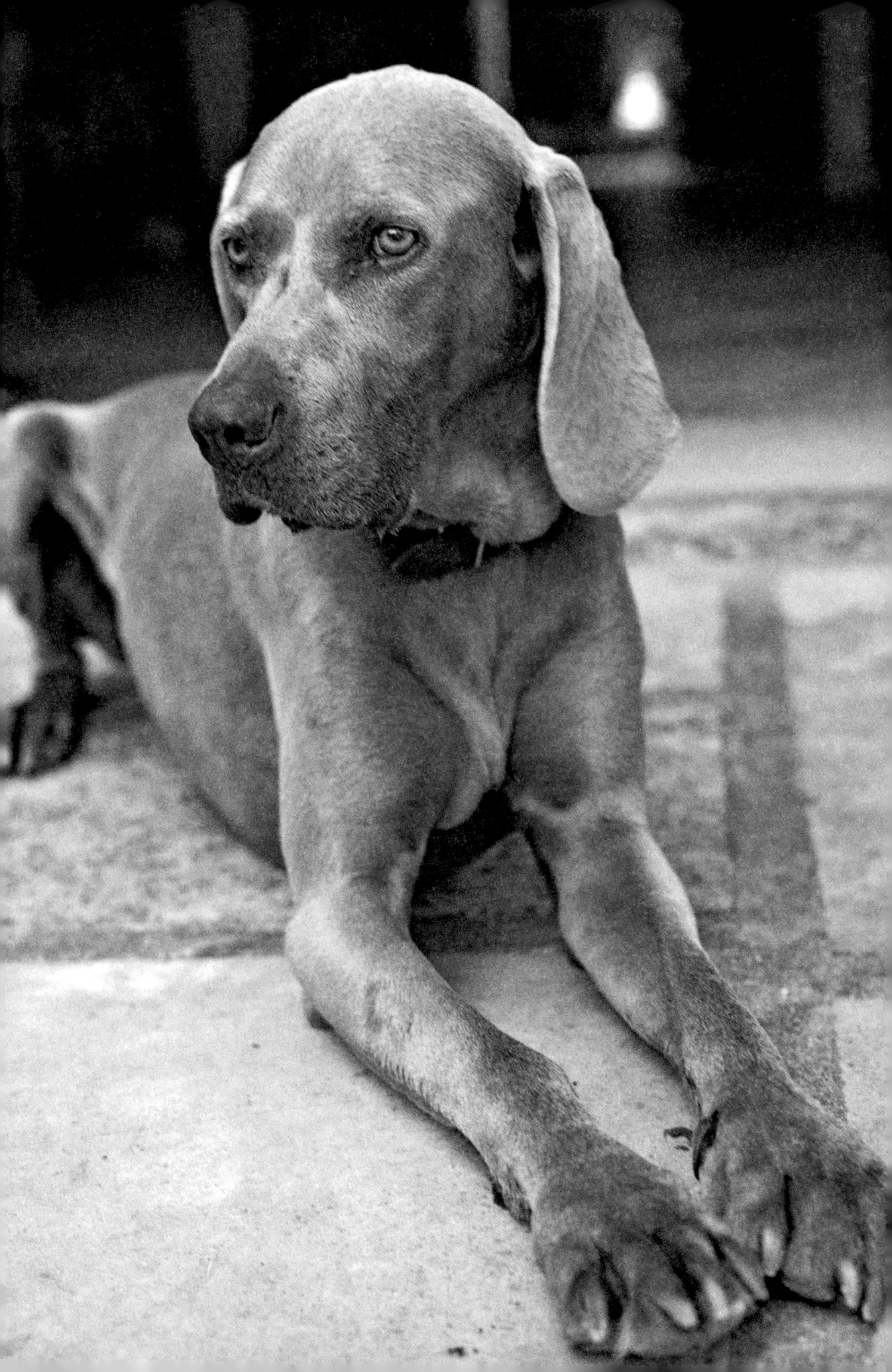

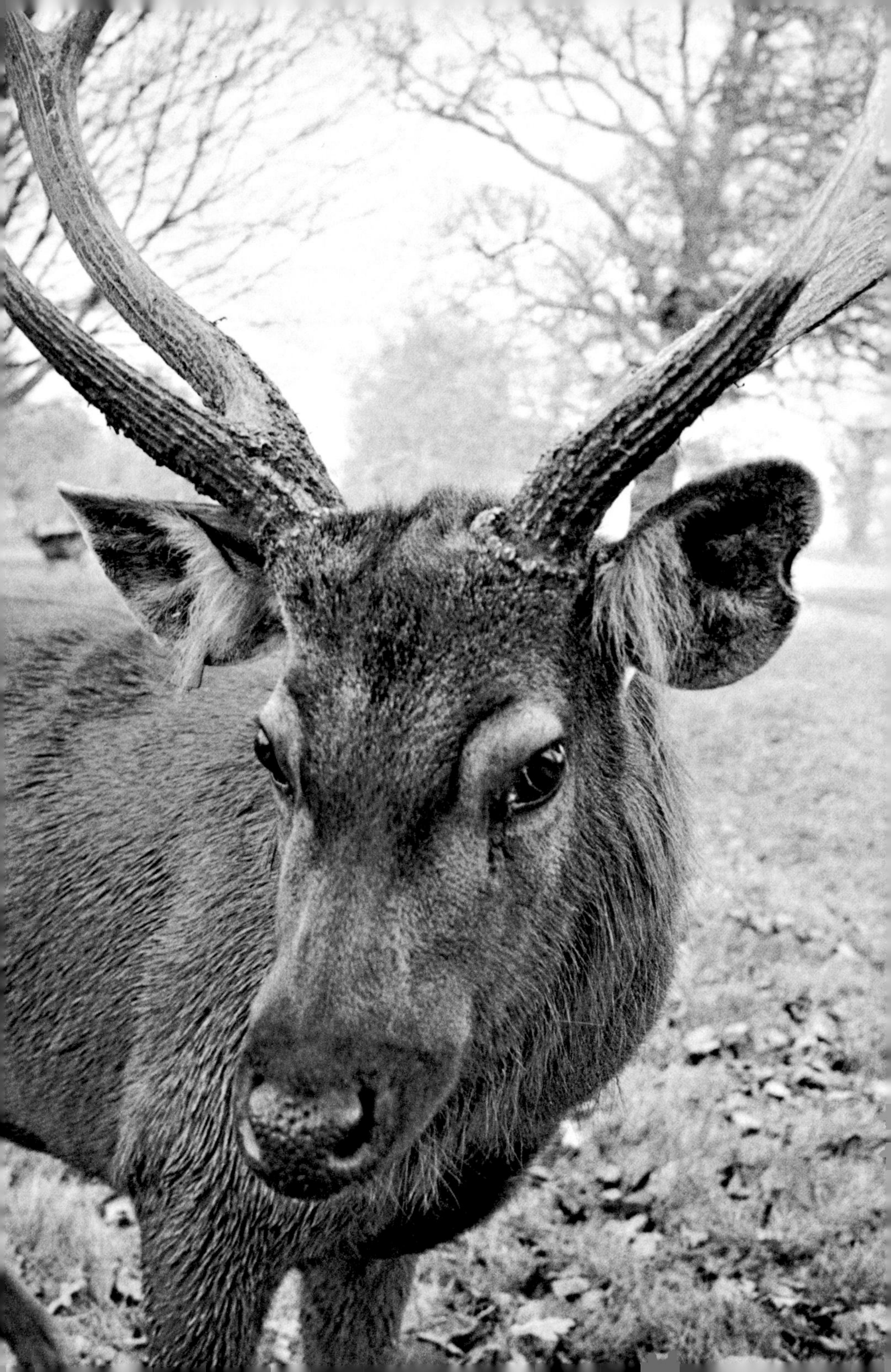

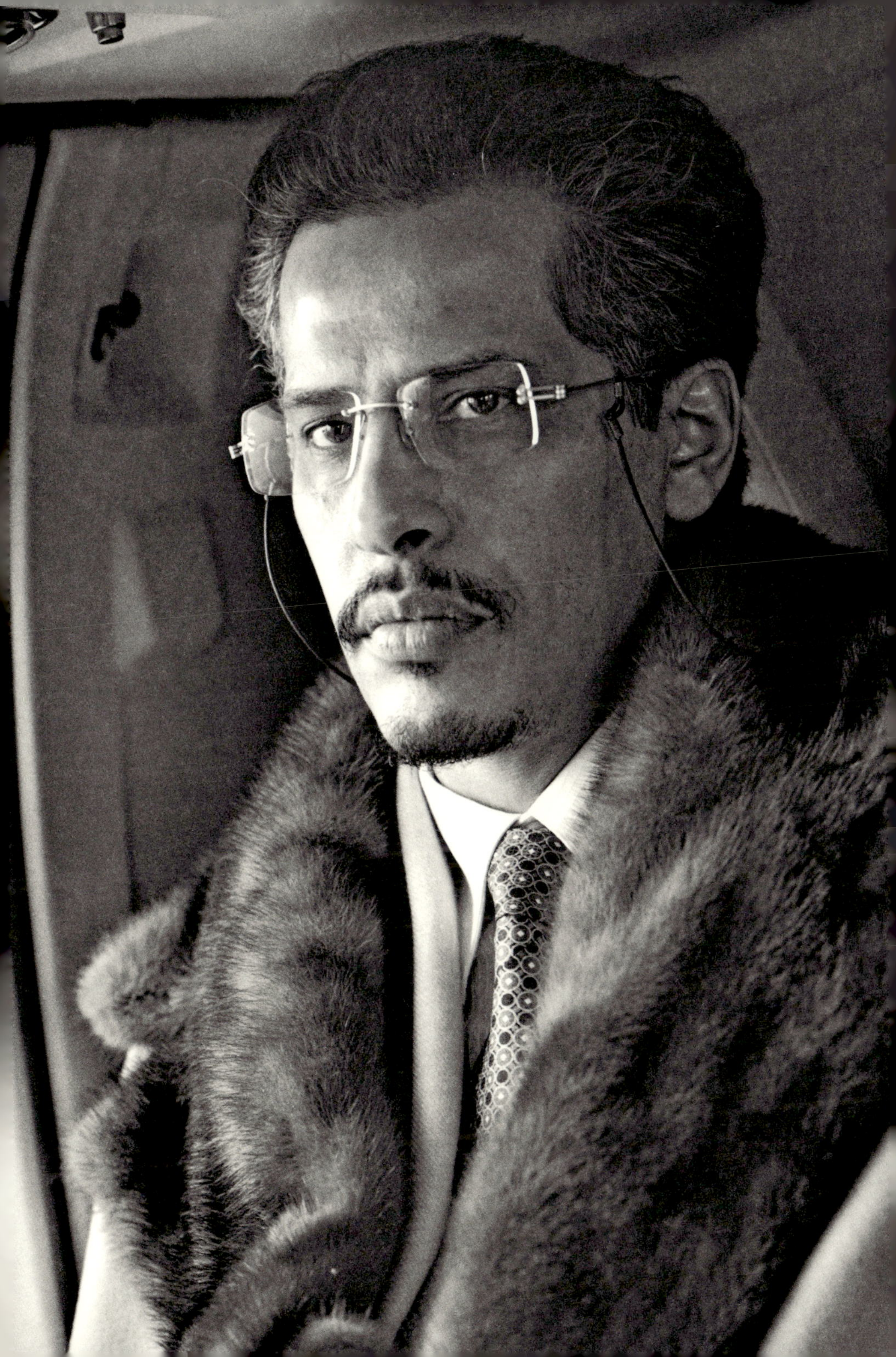

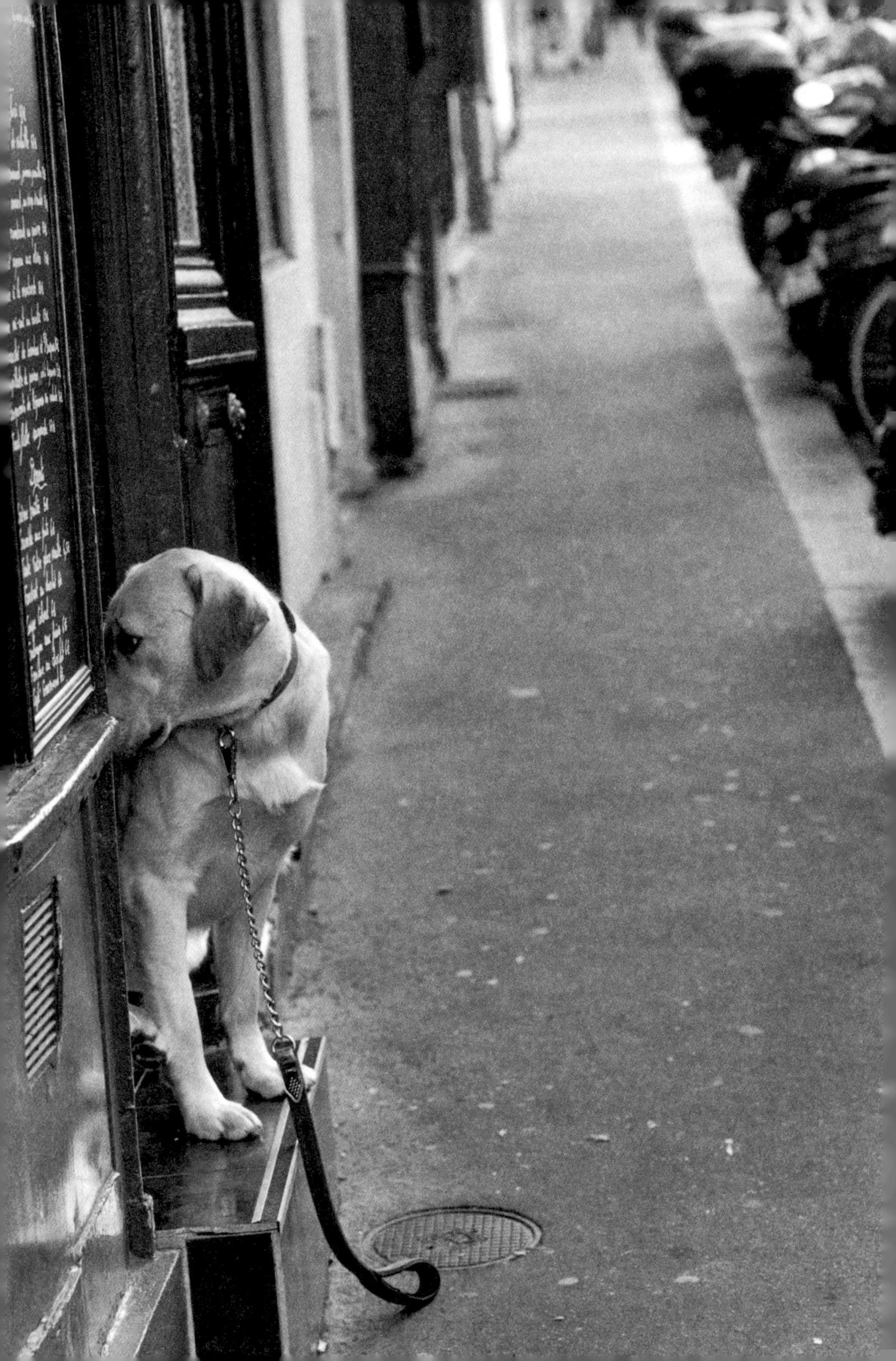

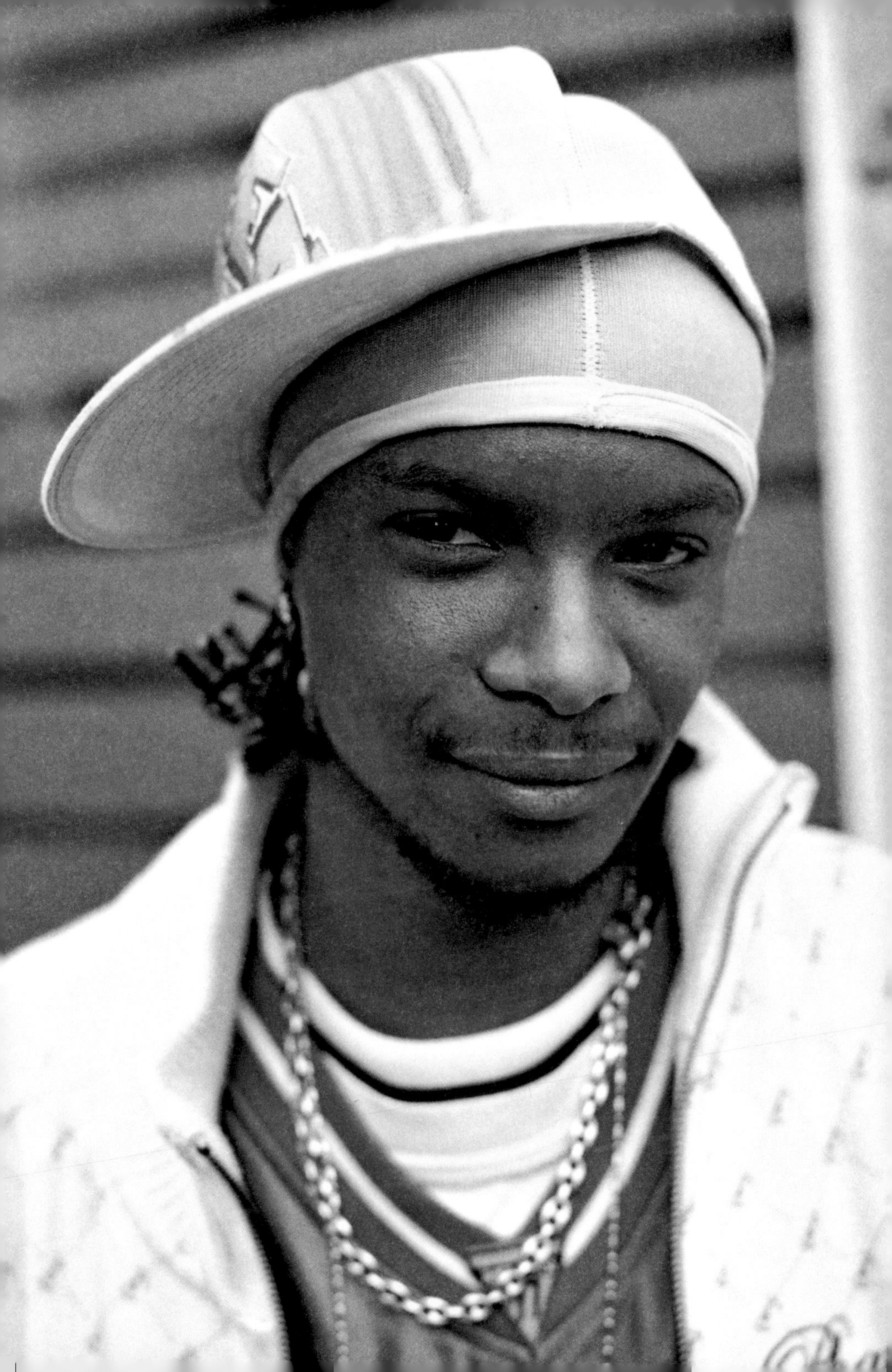

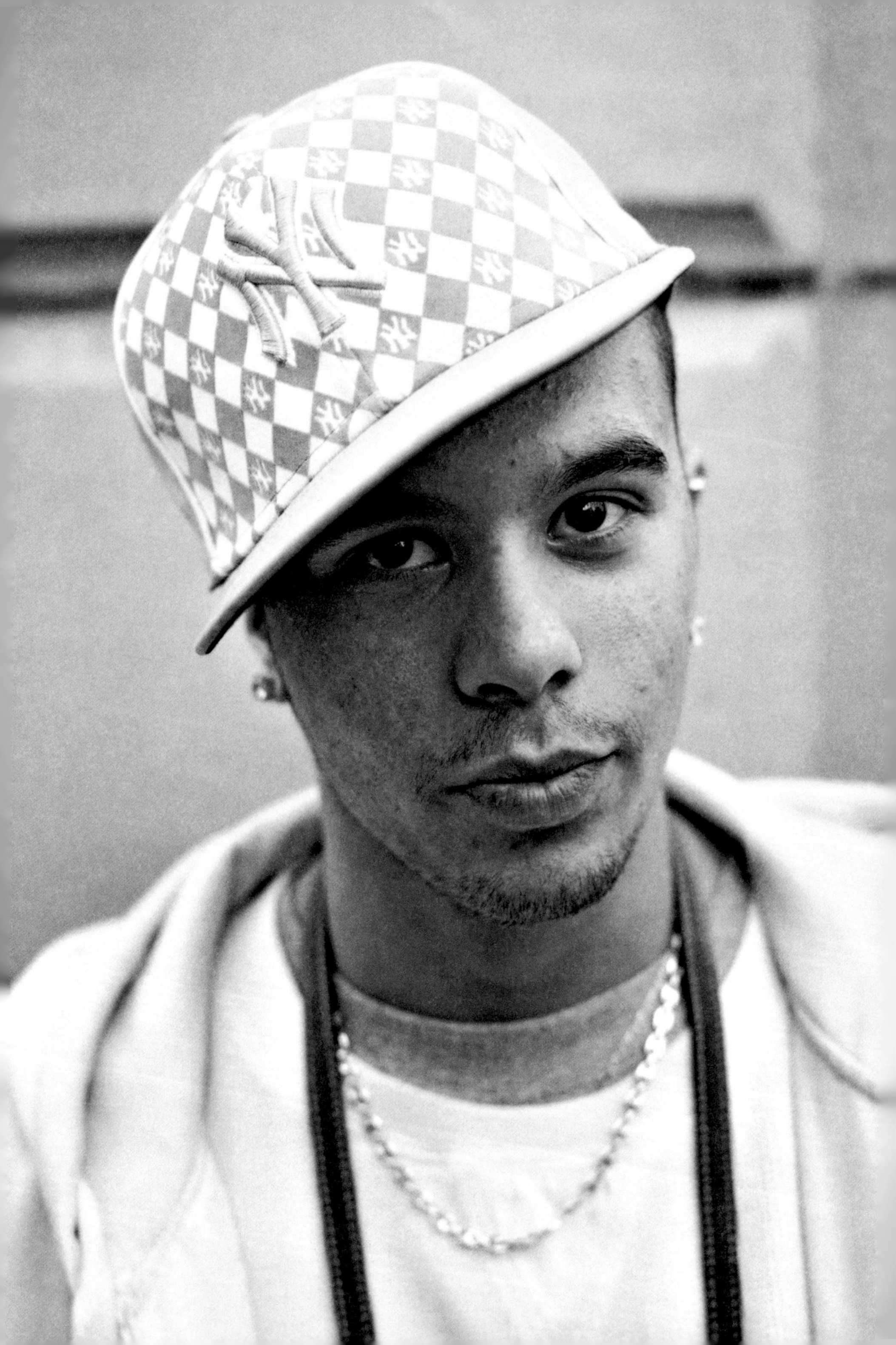

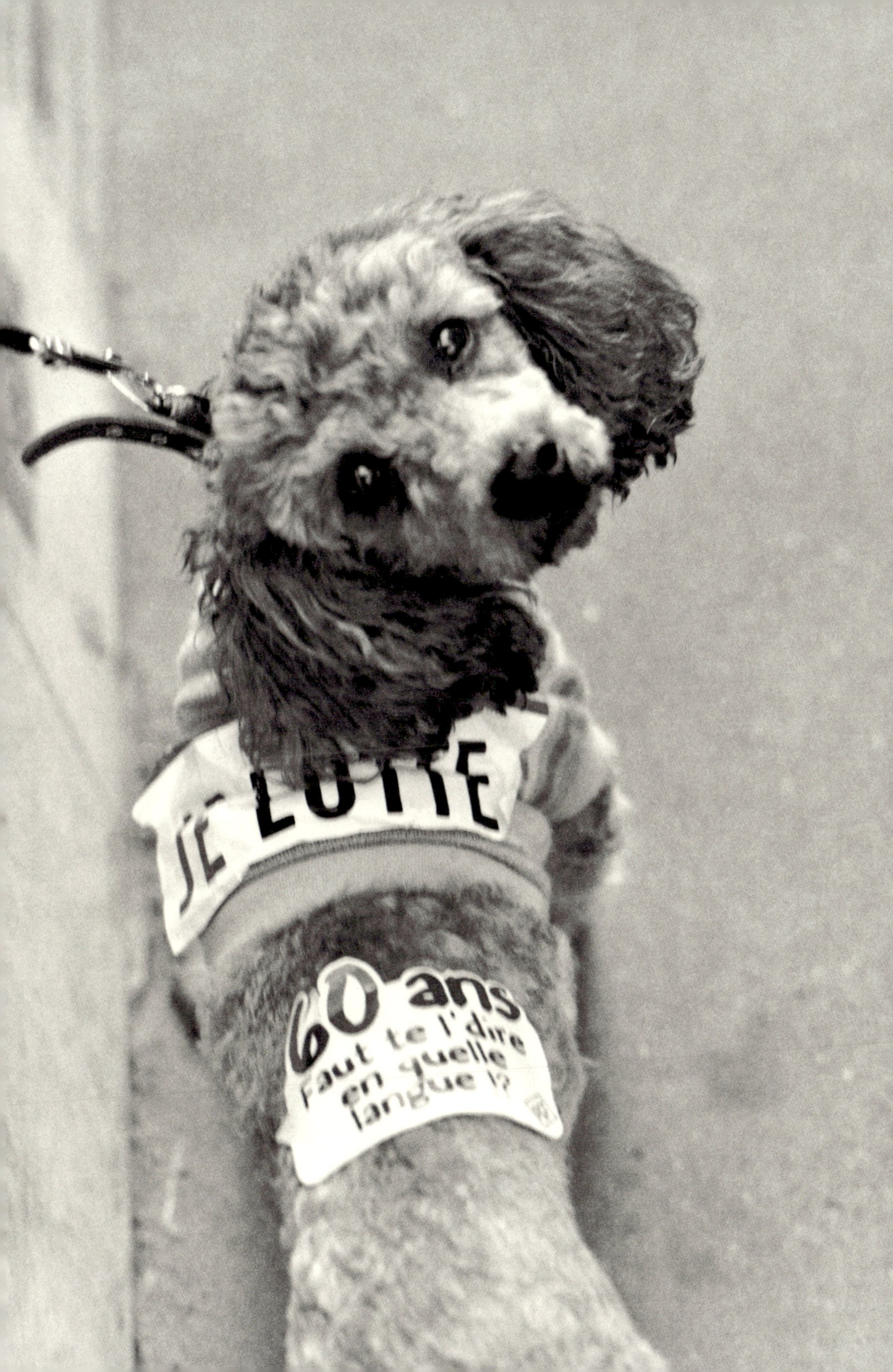
JE LUTTE
60 ans
faut te l'dire
en quelle
langue !?

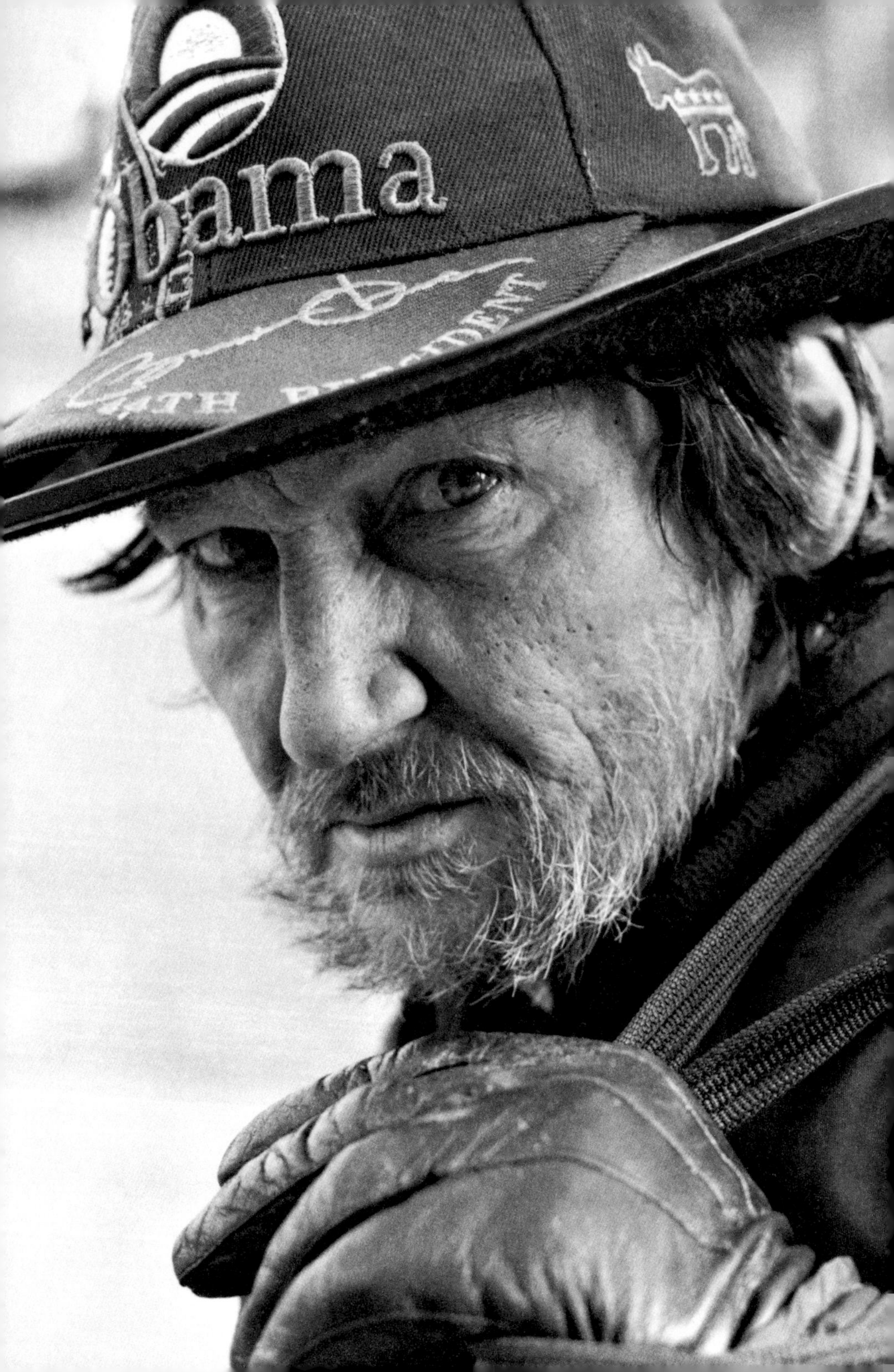
Obama
44TH PRESIDENT

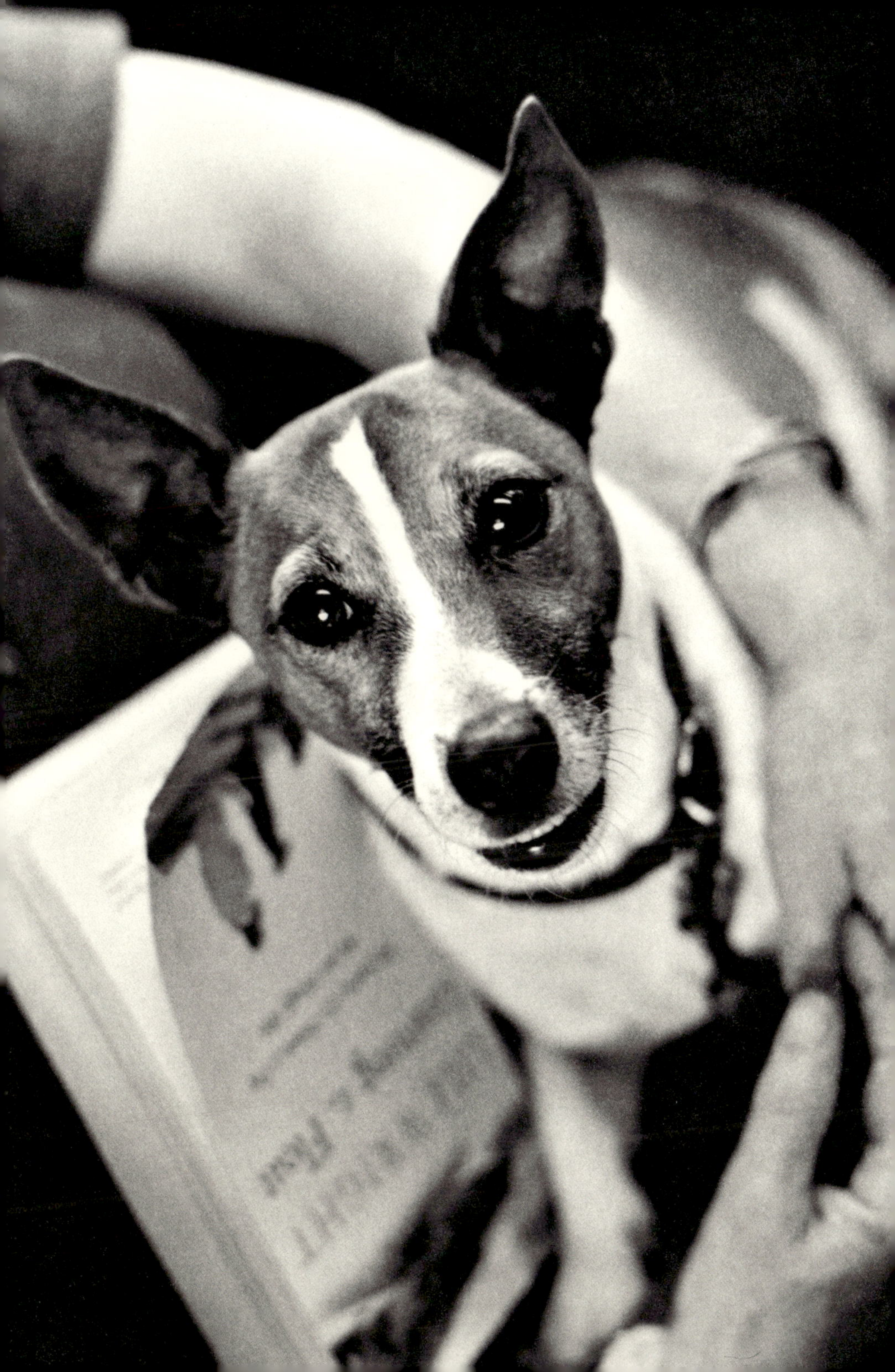

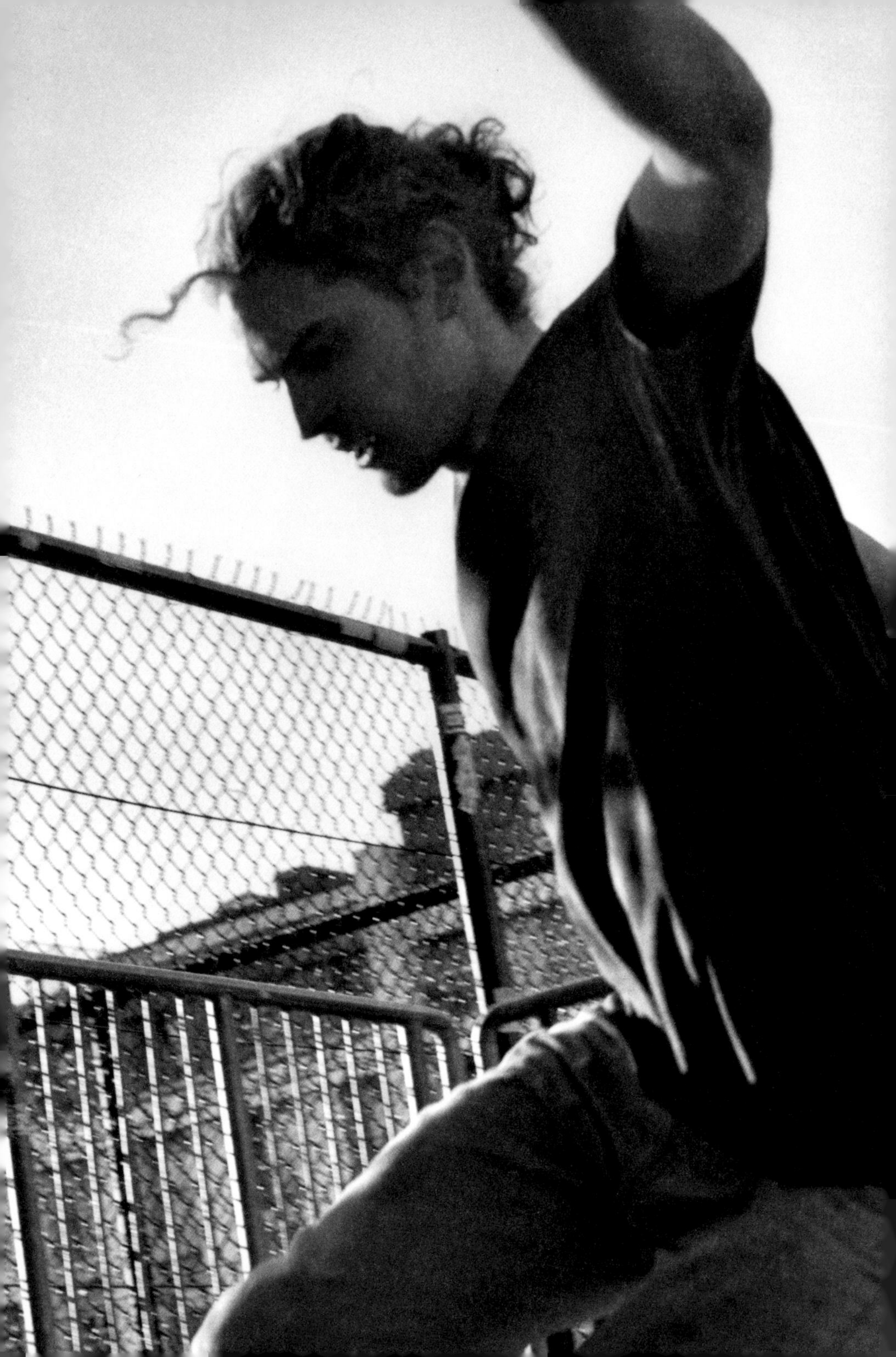

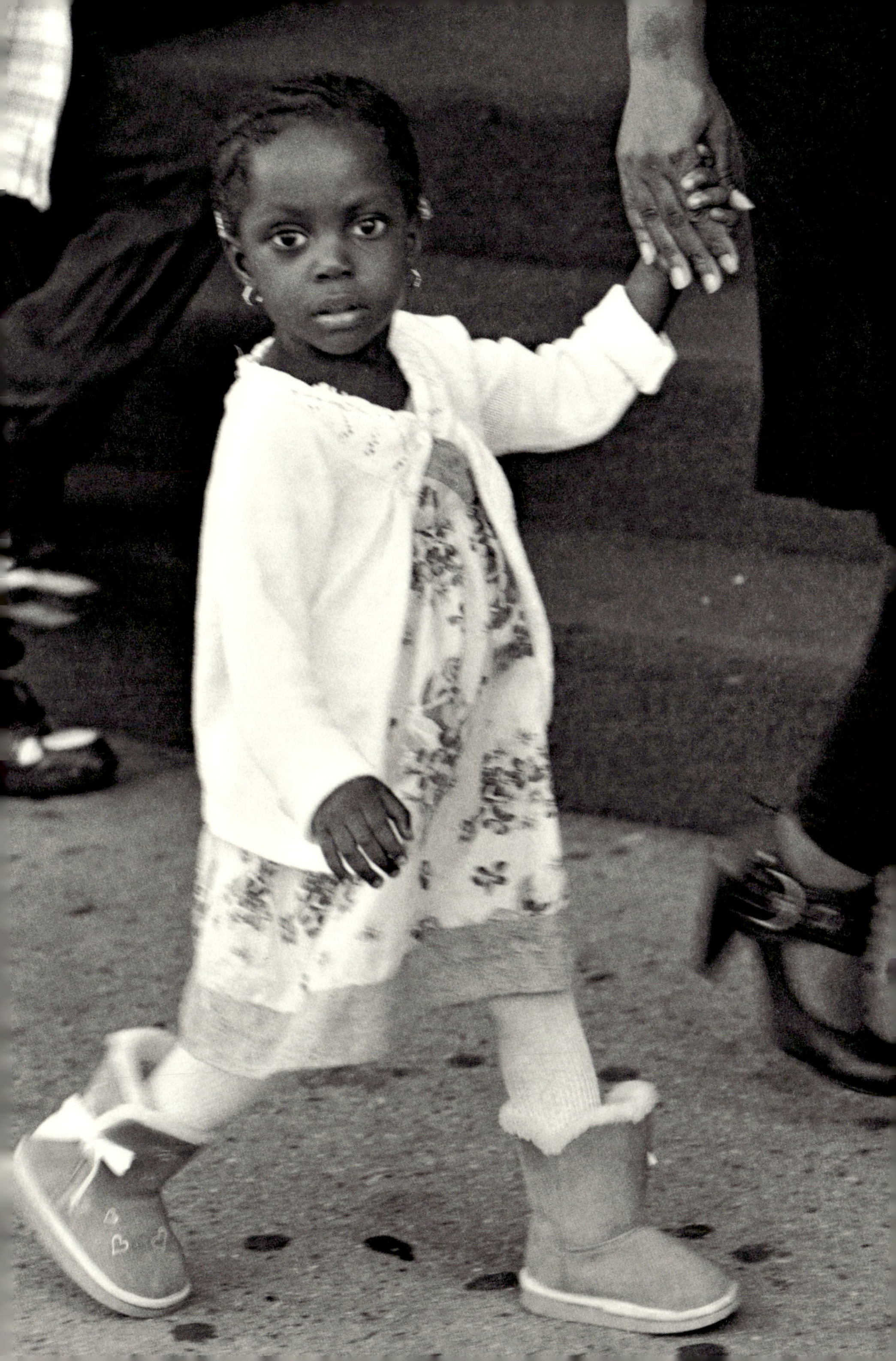

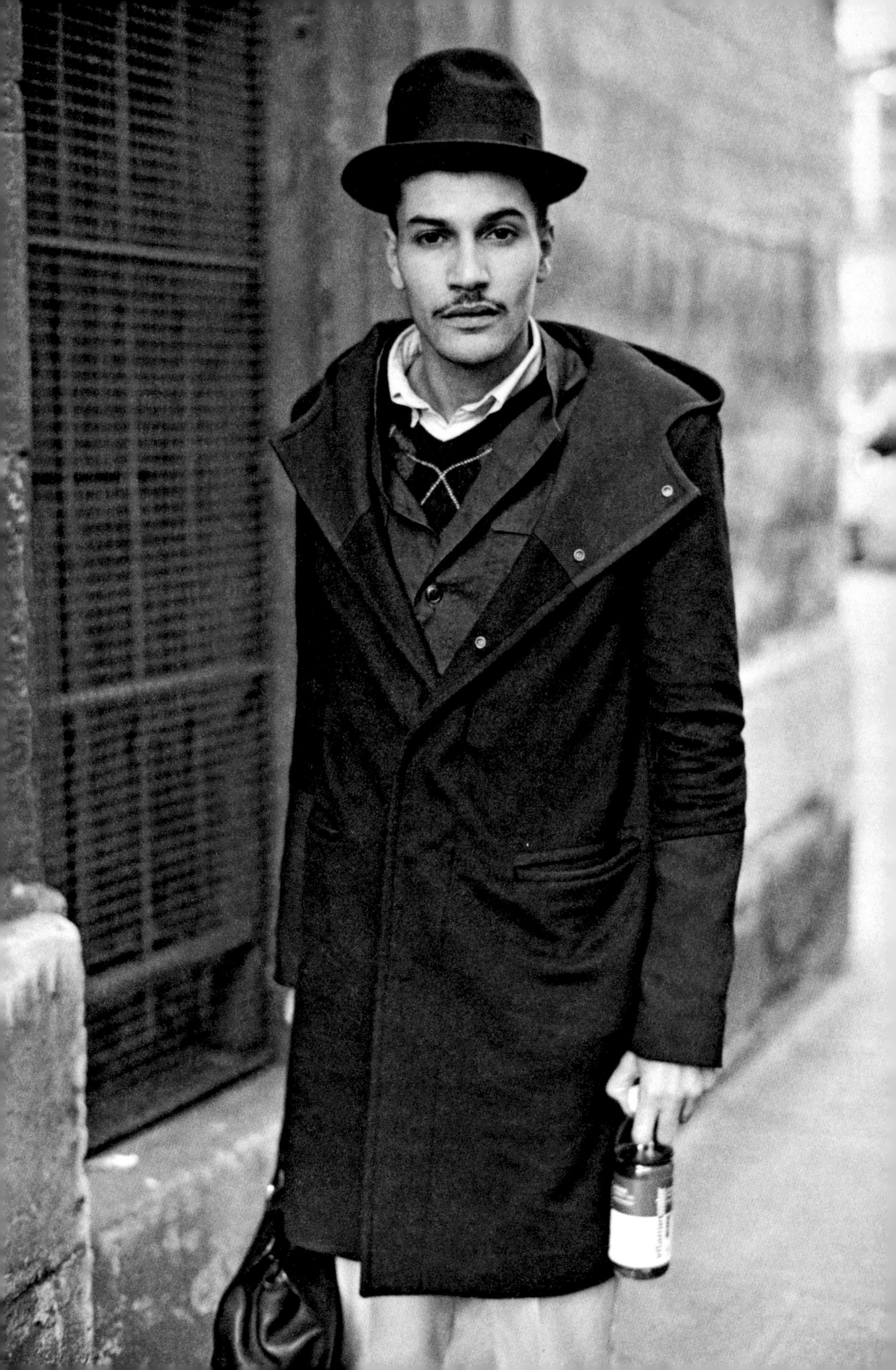

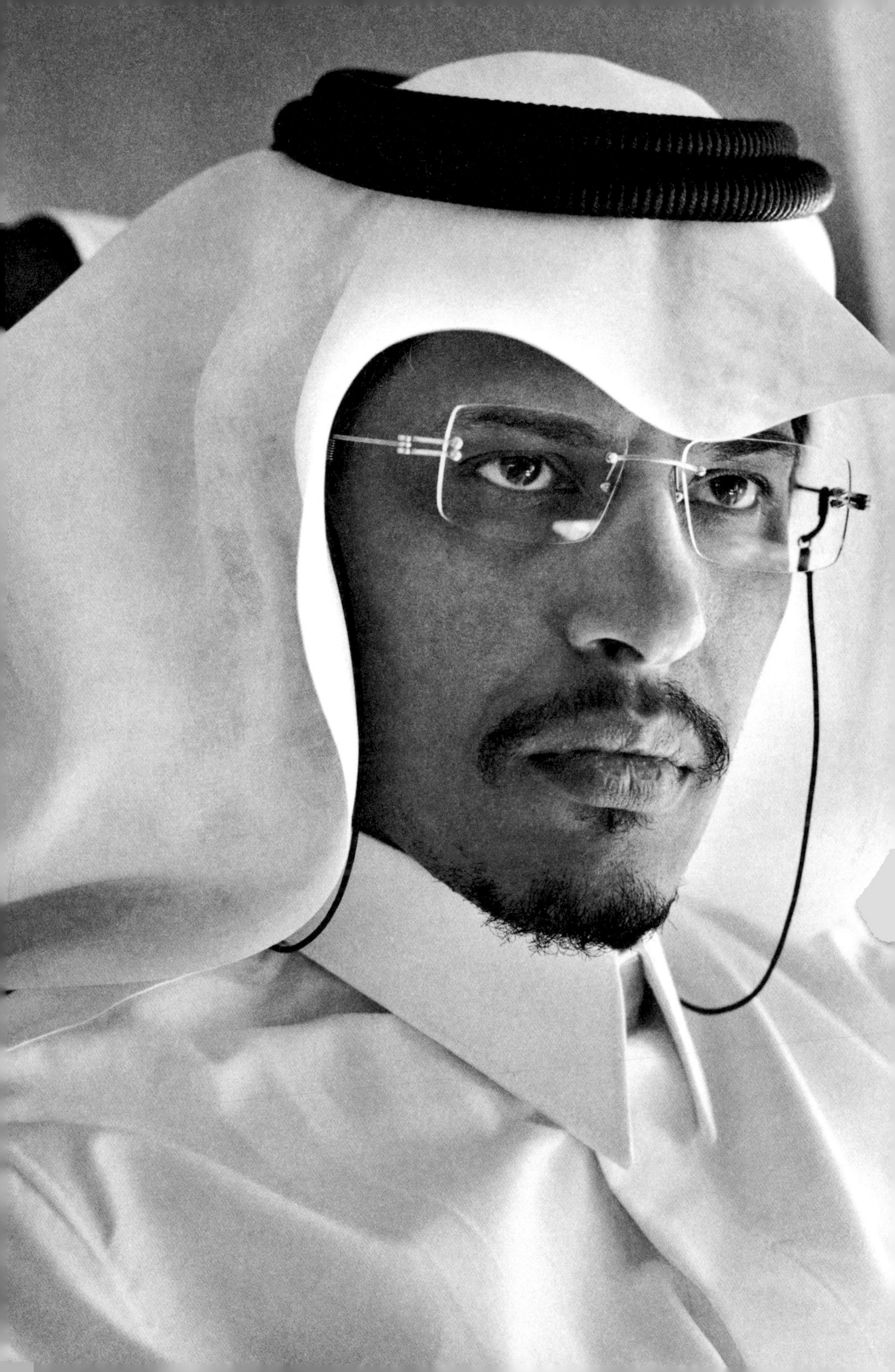

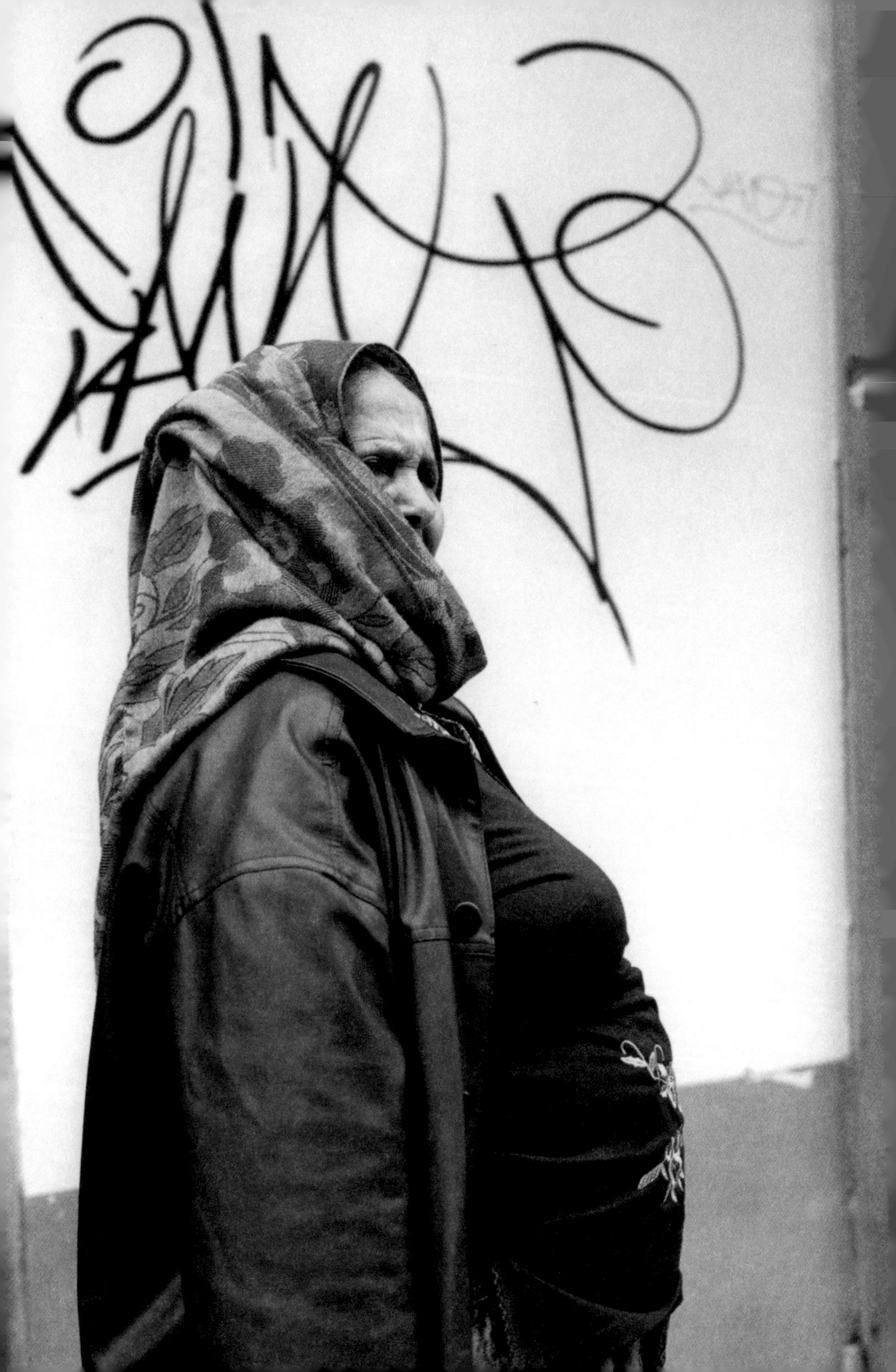

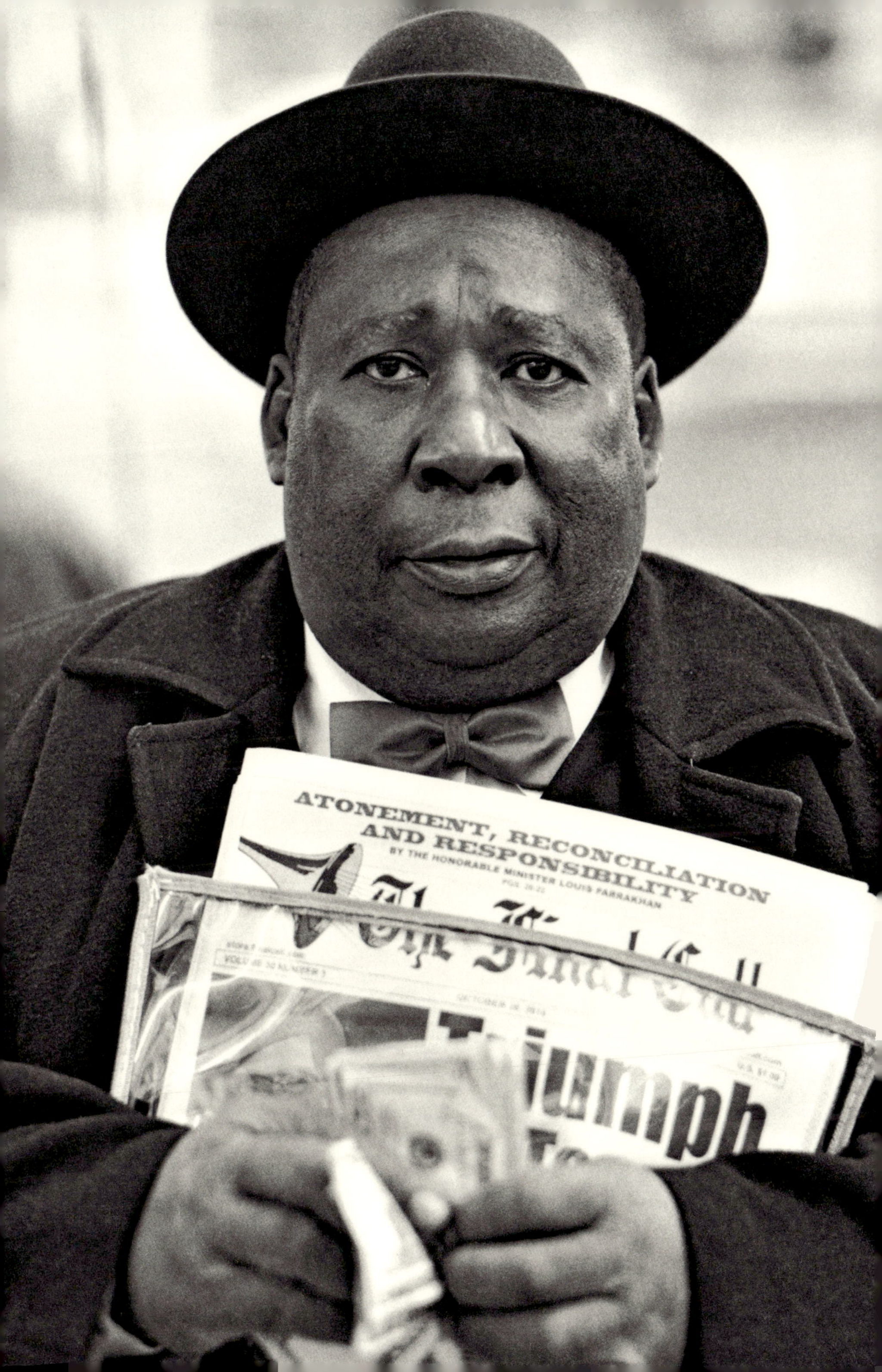

ATONEMENT, RECONCILIATION AND RESPONSIBILITY
BY THE HONORABLE MINISTER LOUIS FARRAKHAN
Triumph

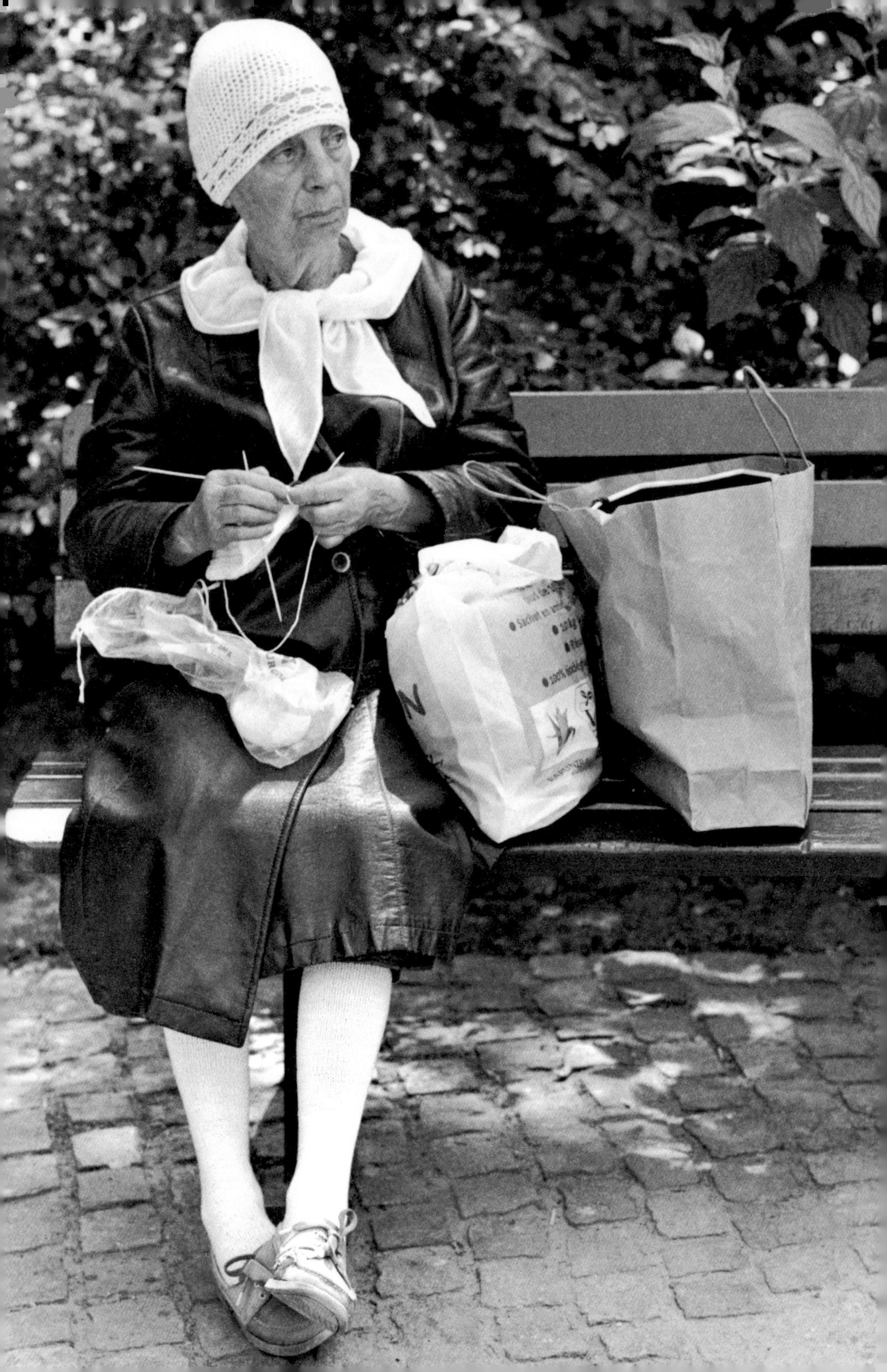

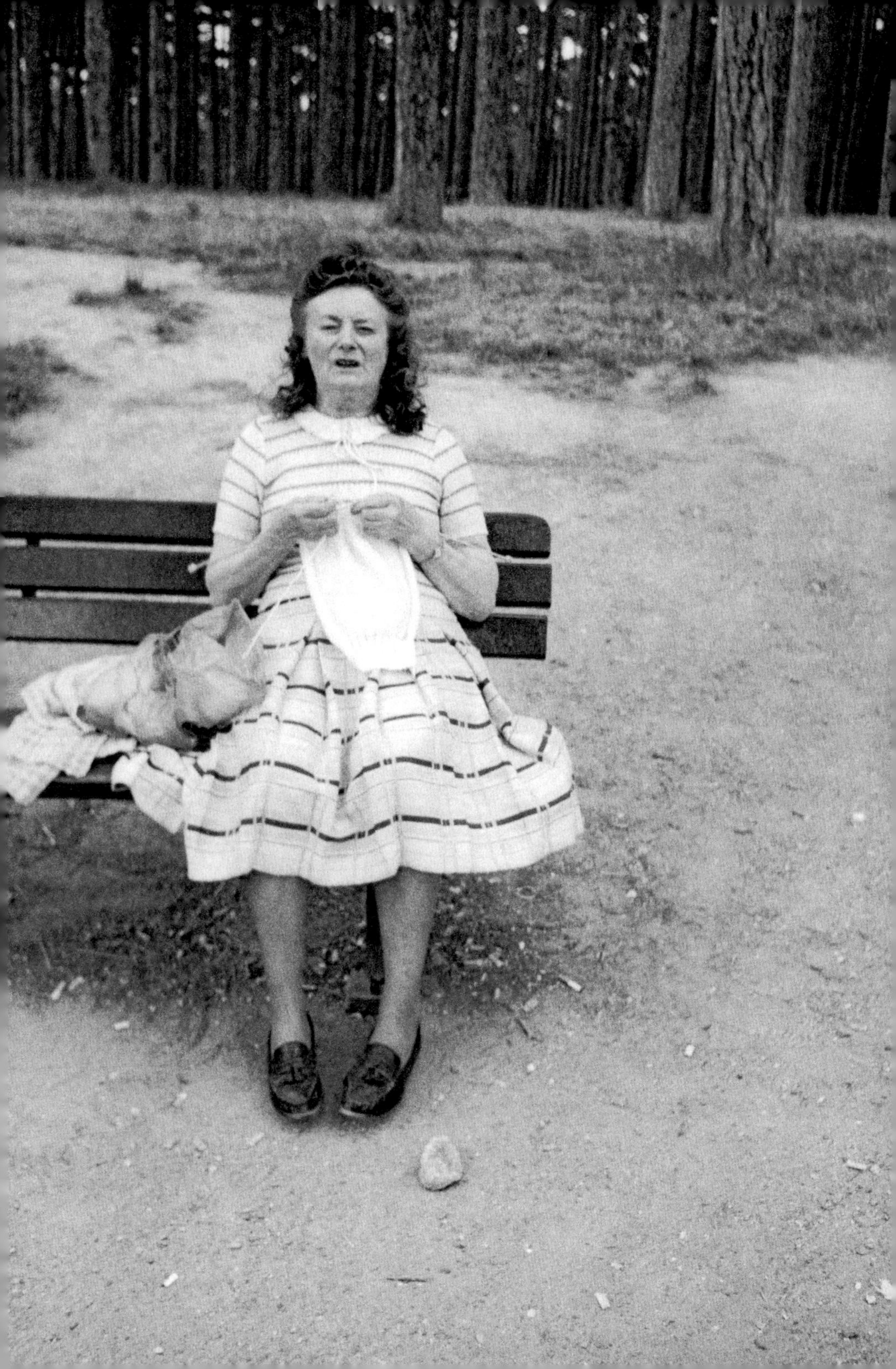

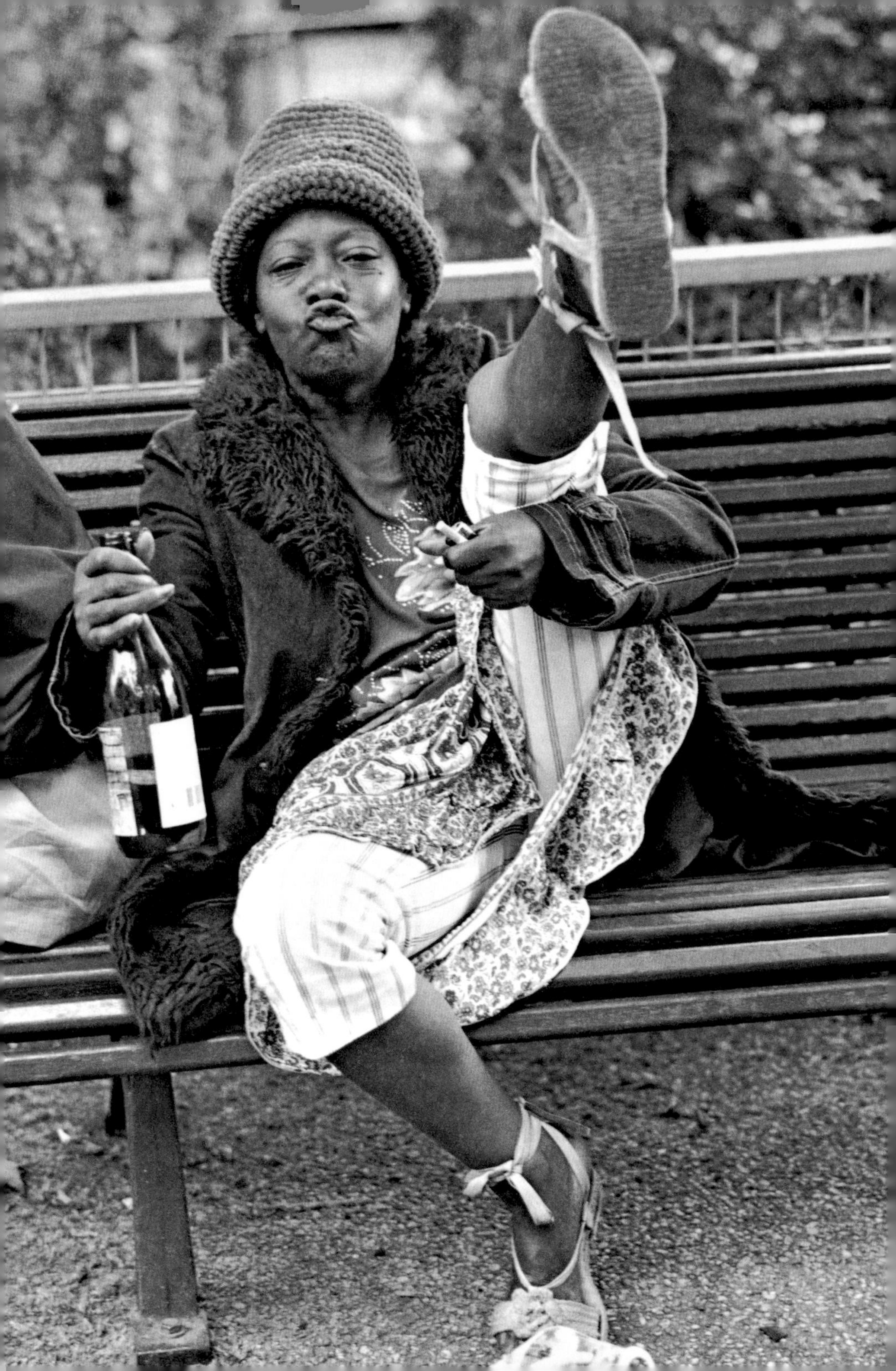

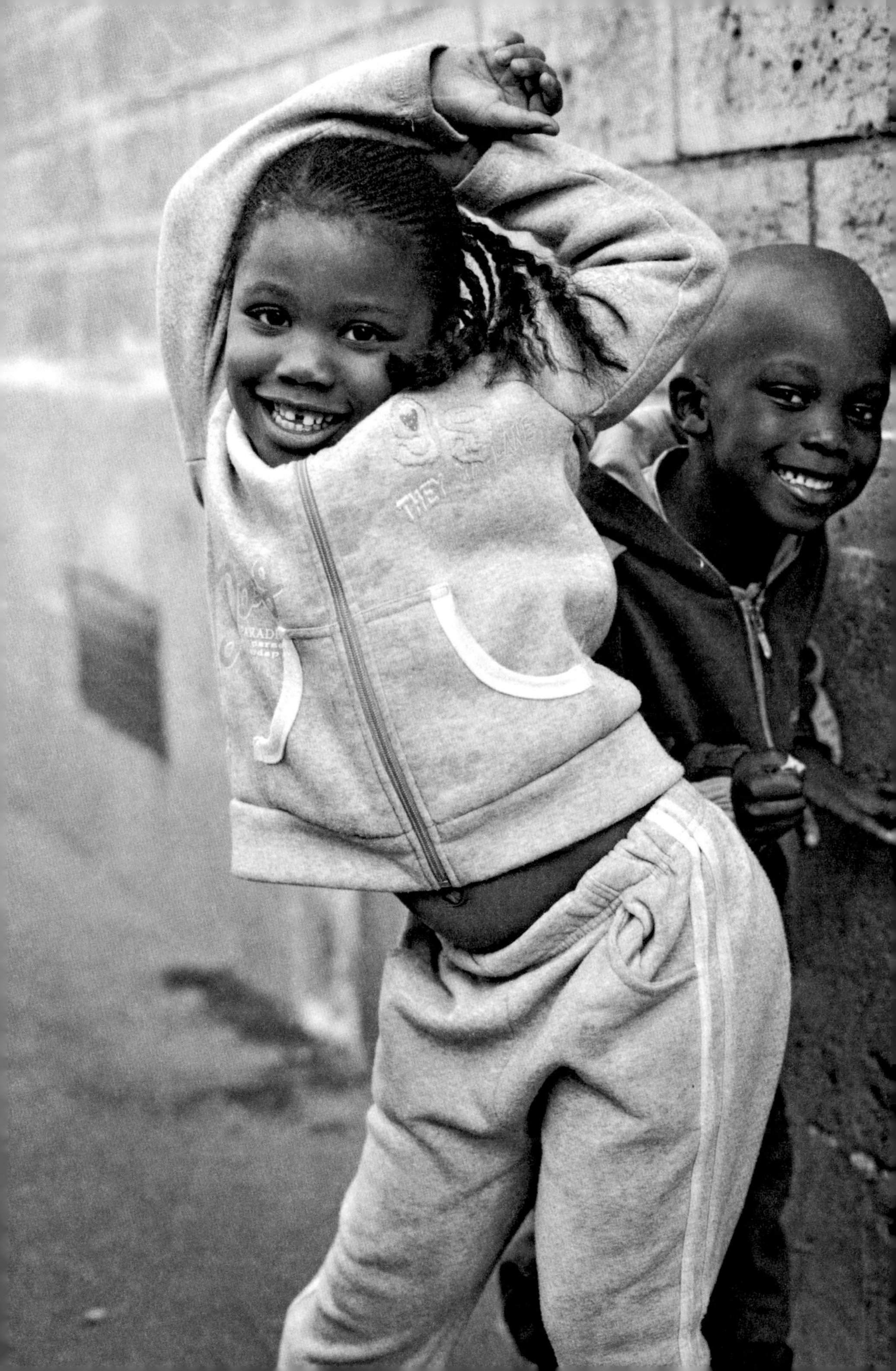

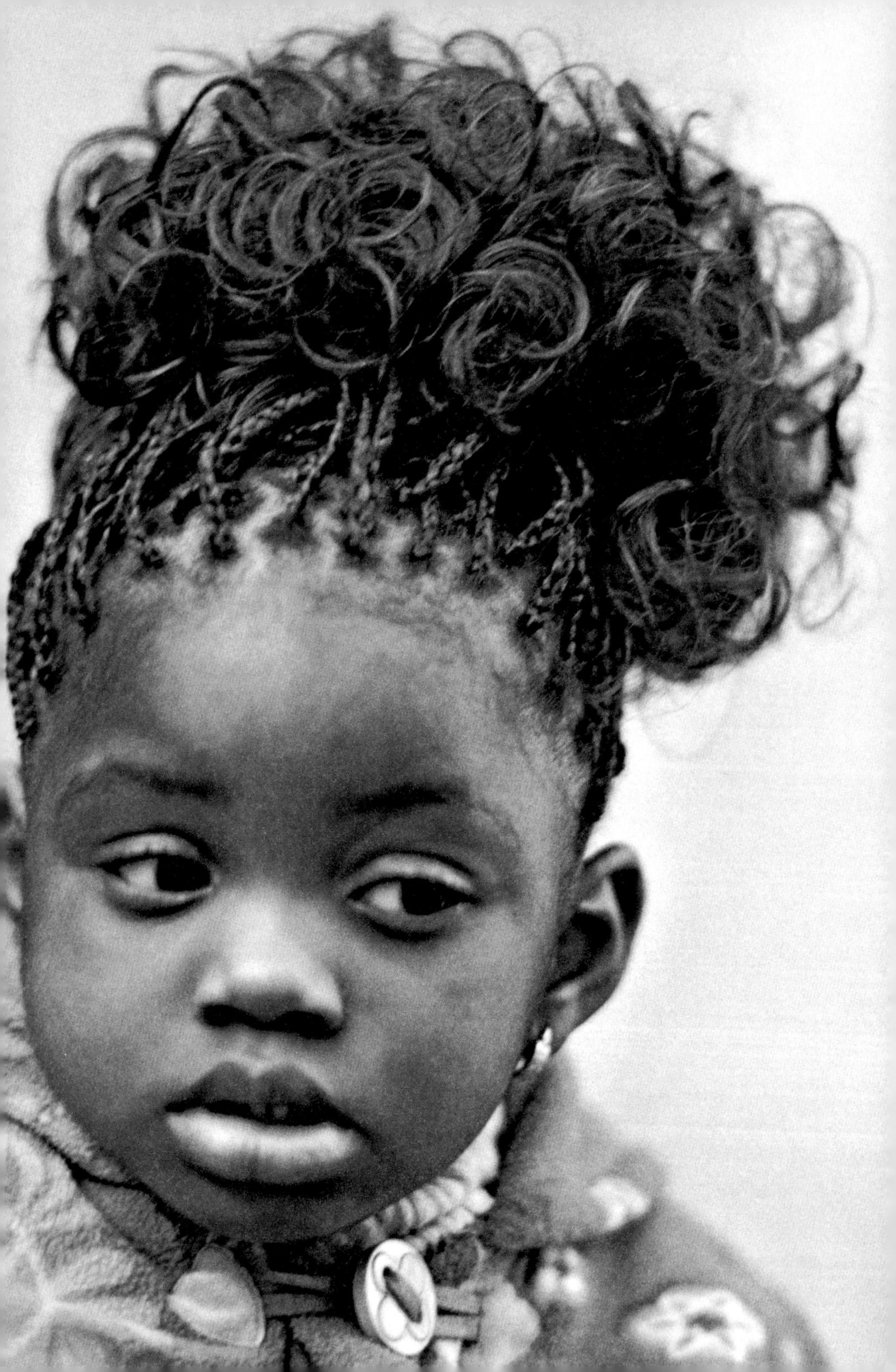

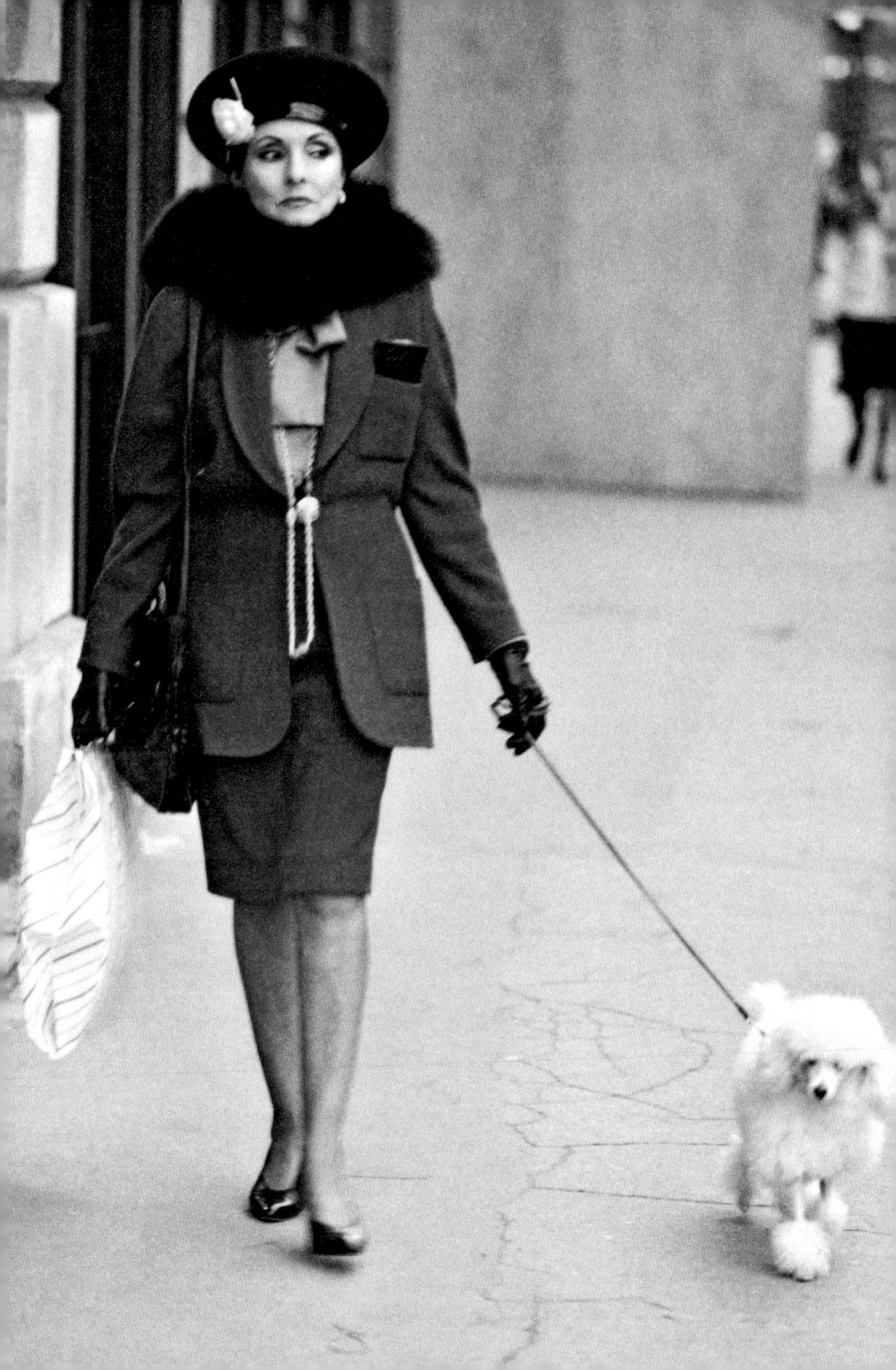

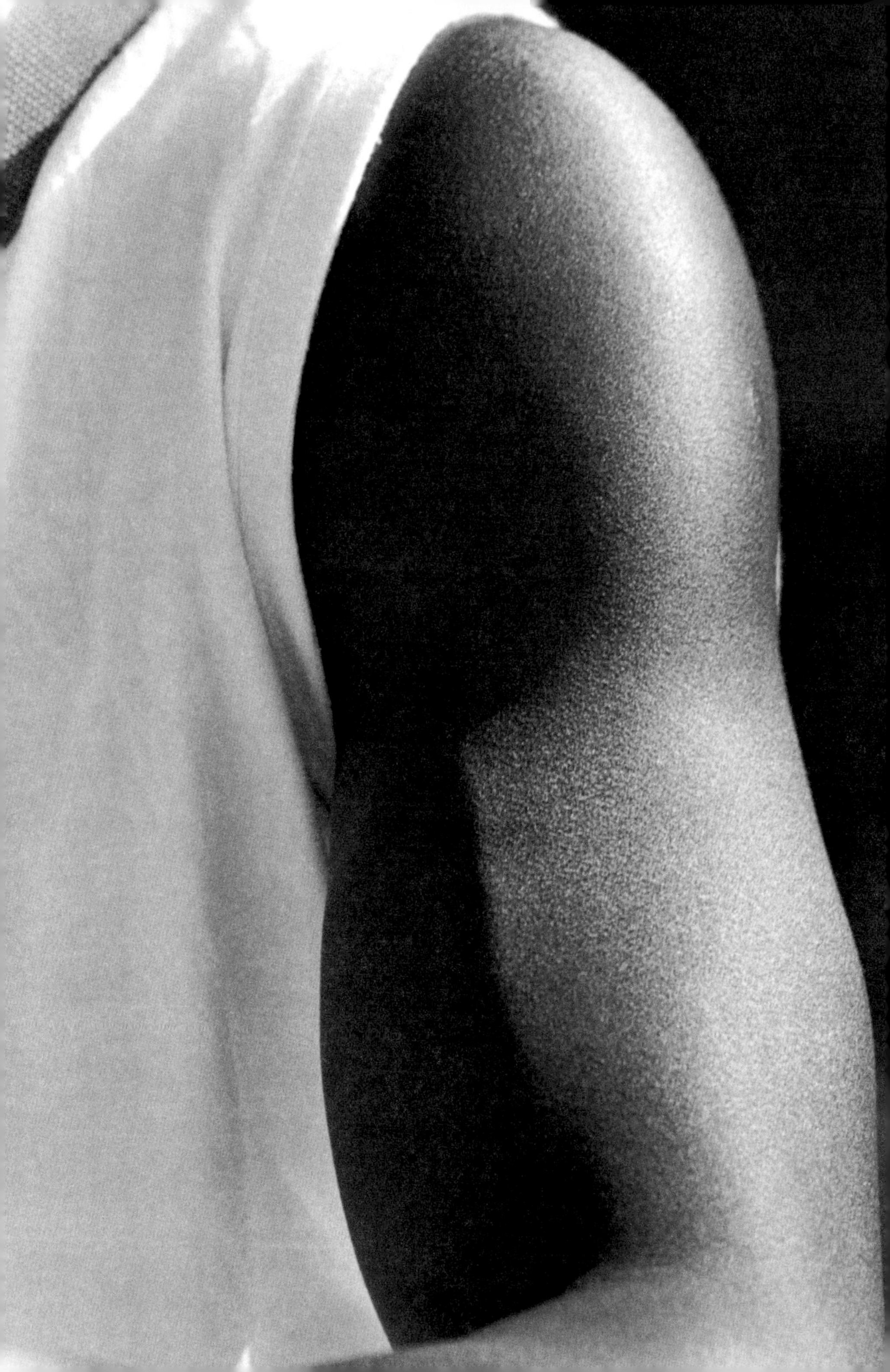

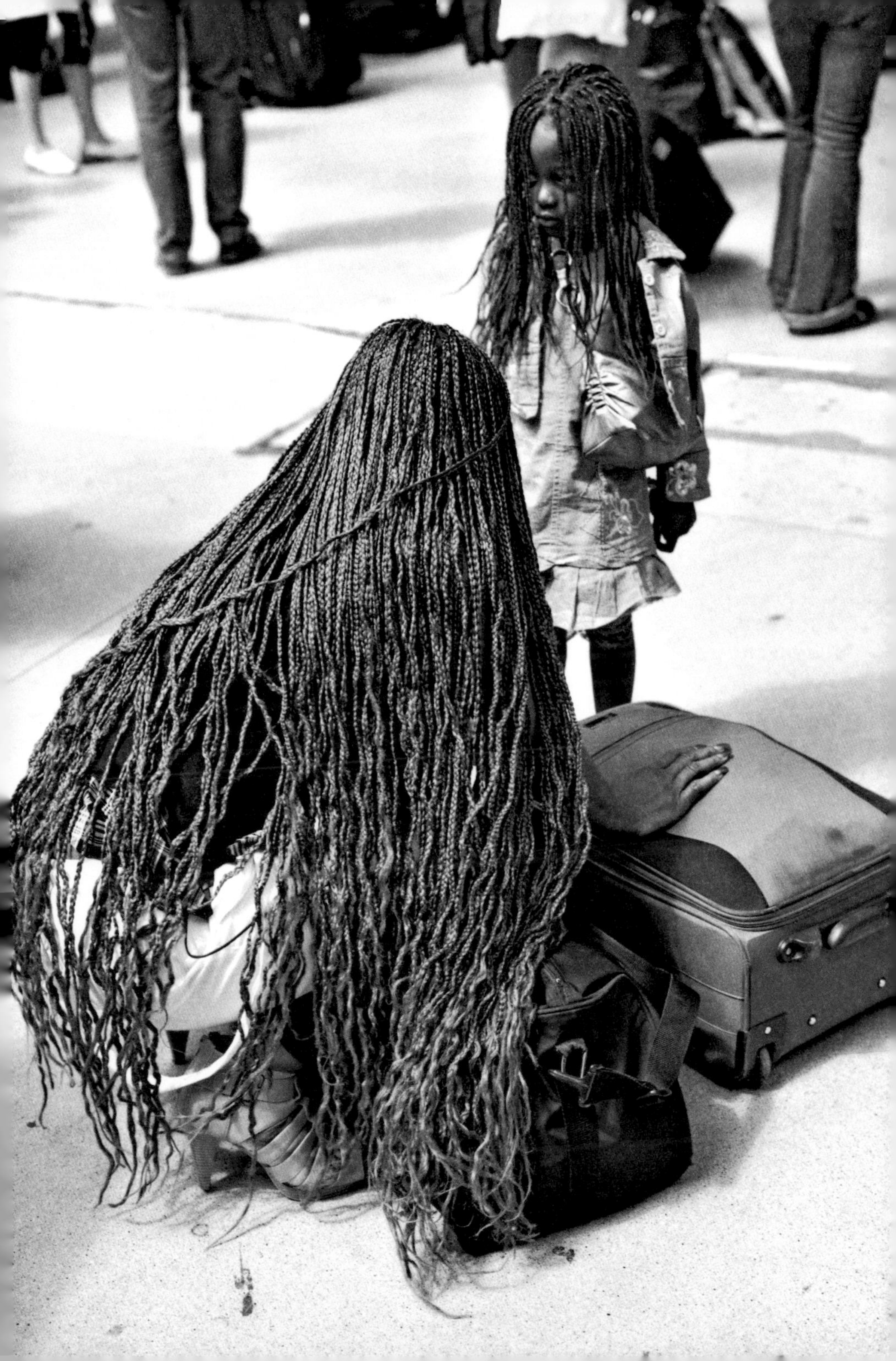

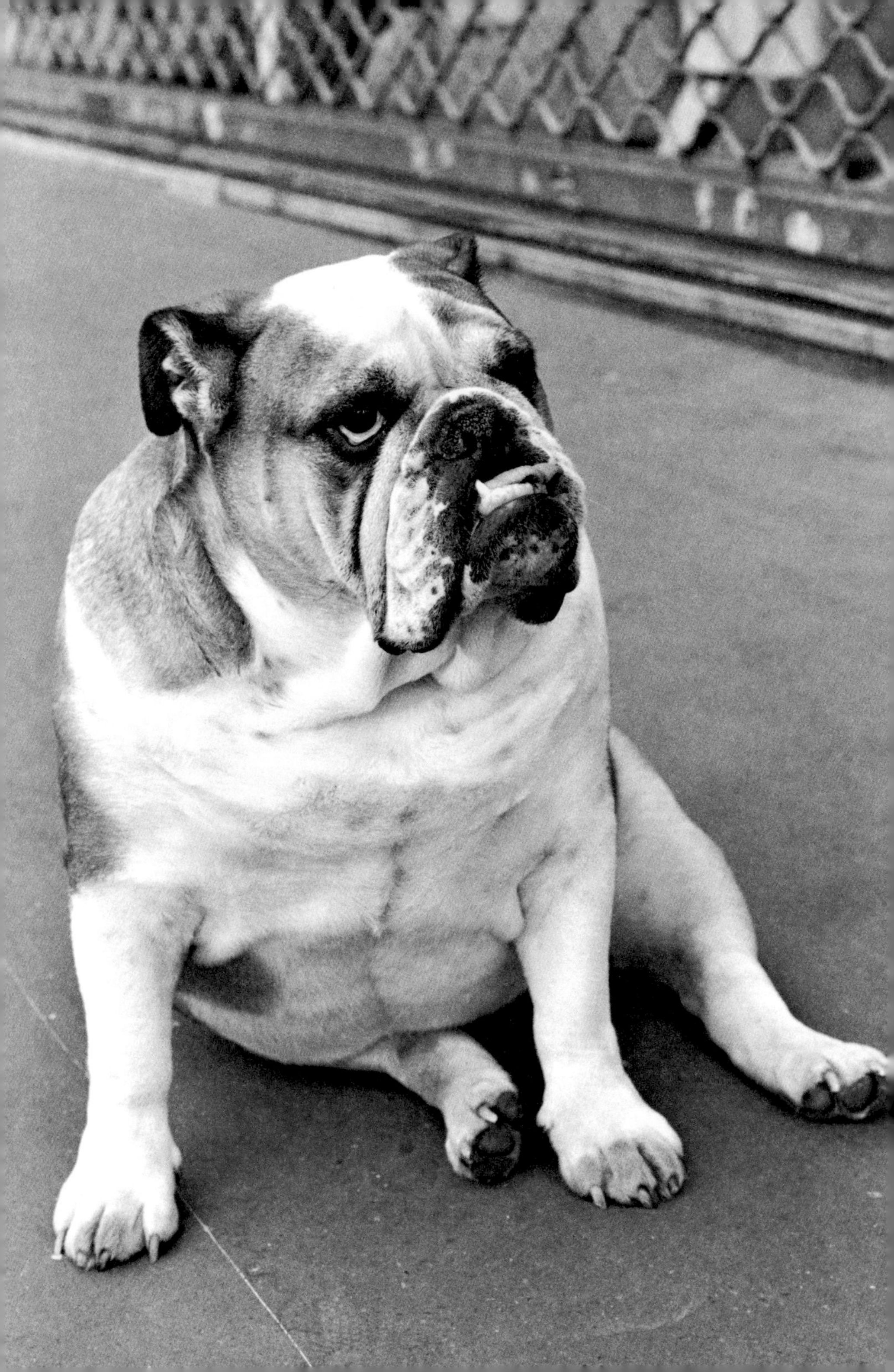

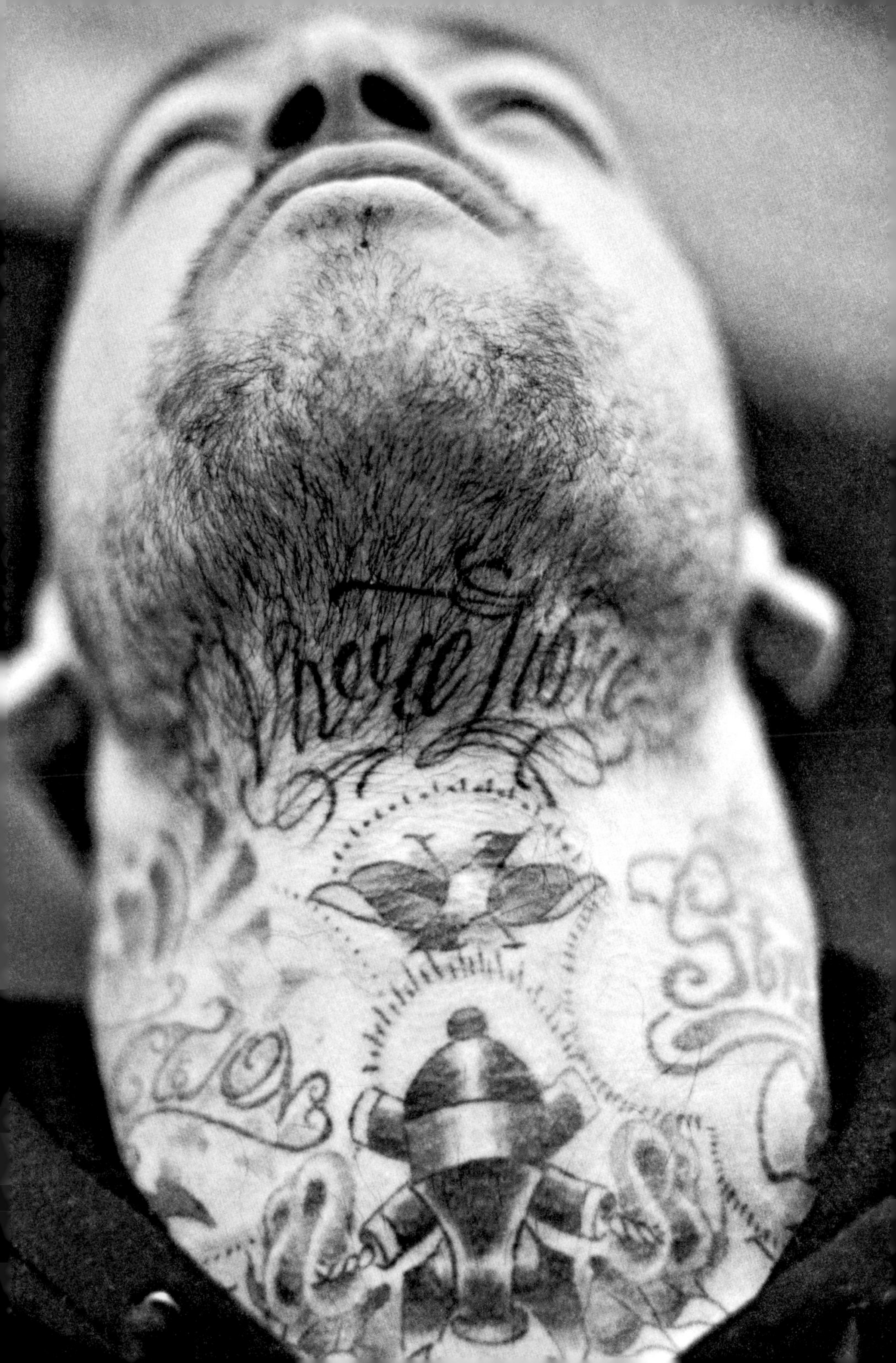

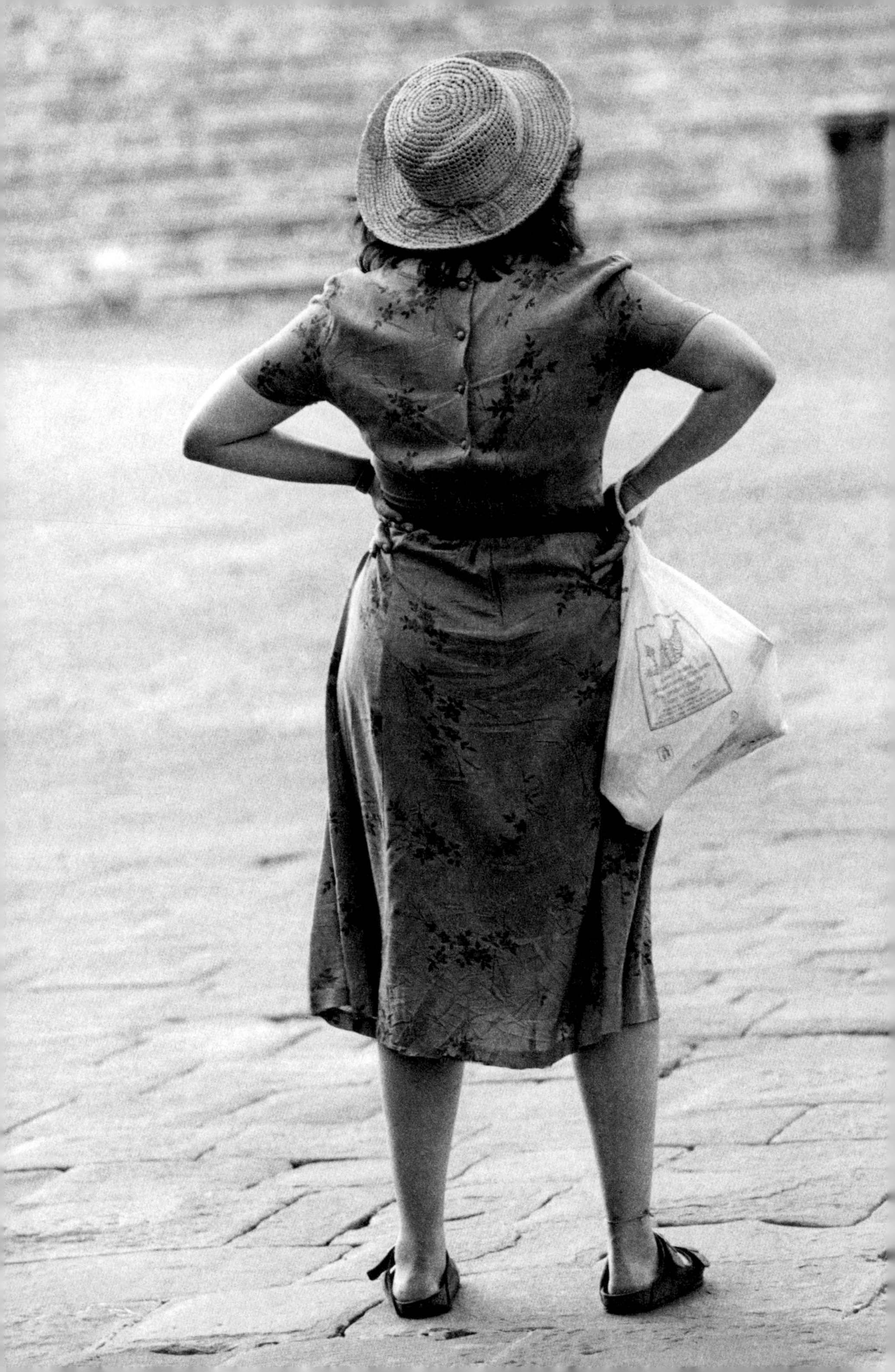

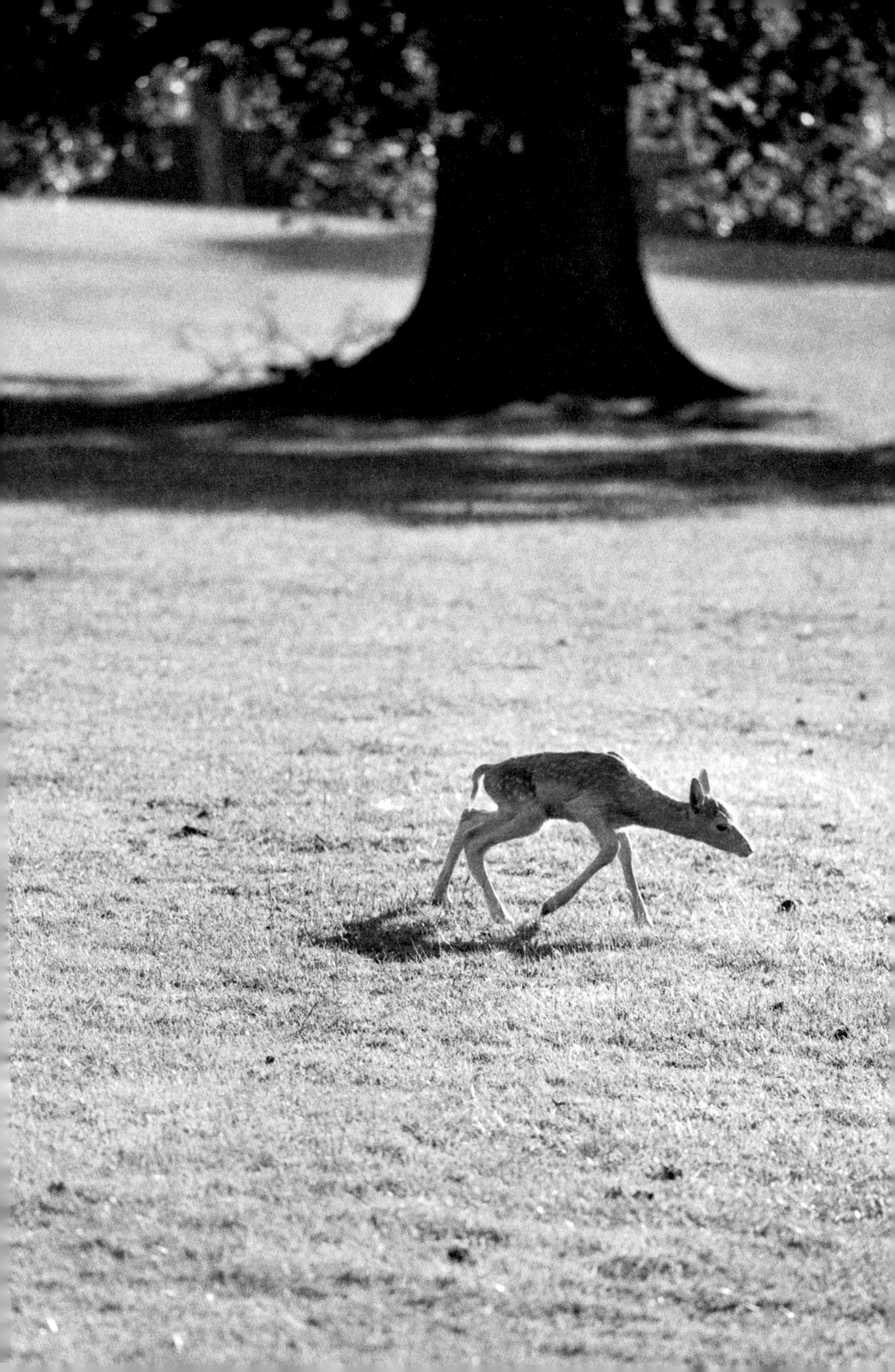

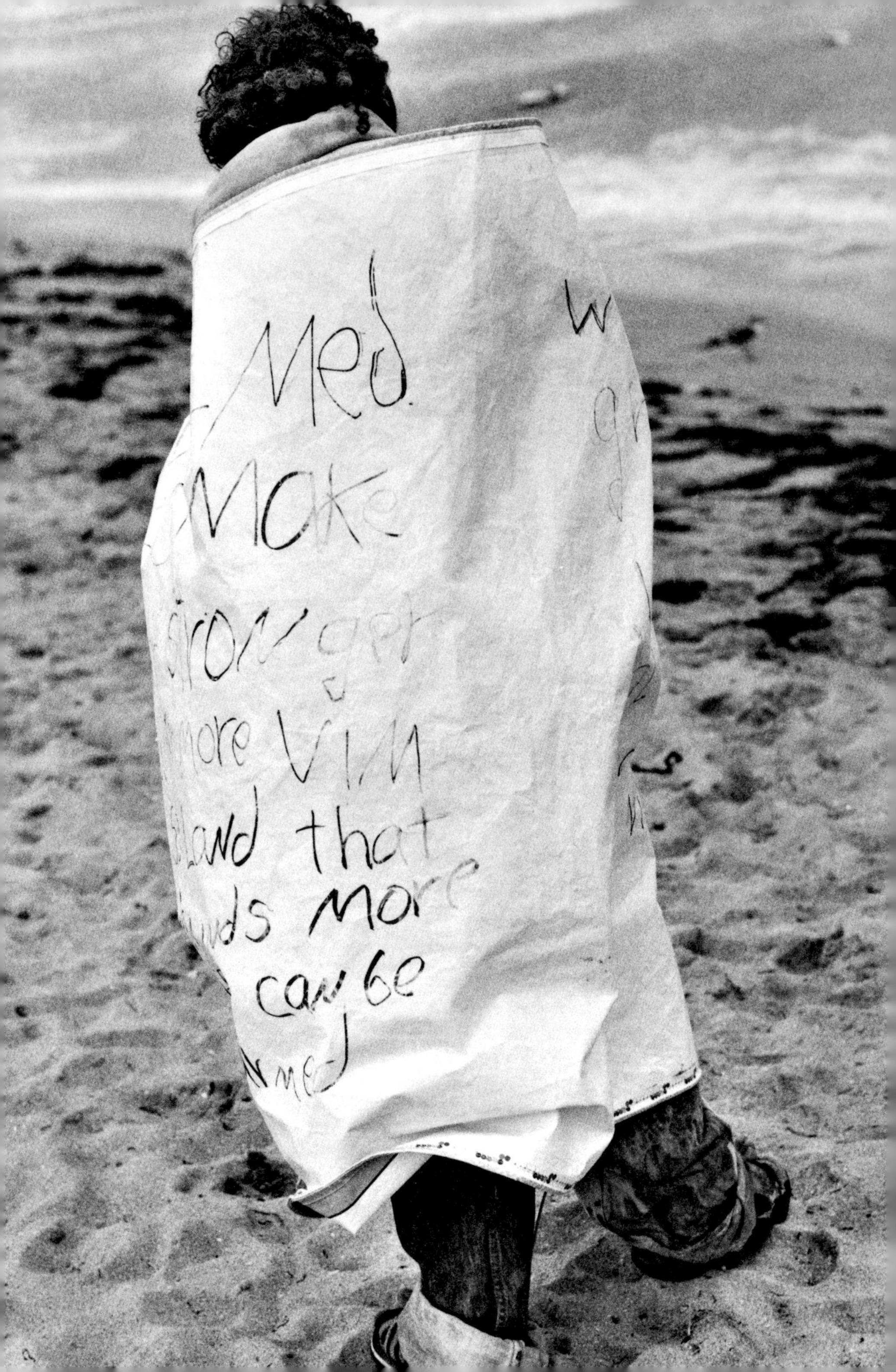
Med.
make
stronger
more vim
and that
ds more
can be
me

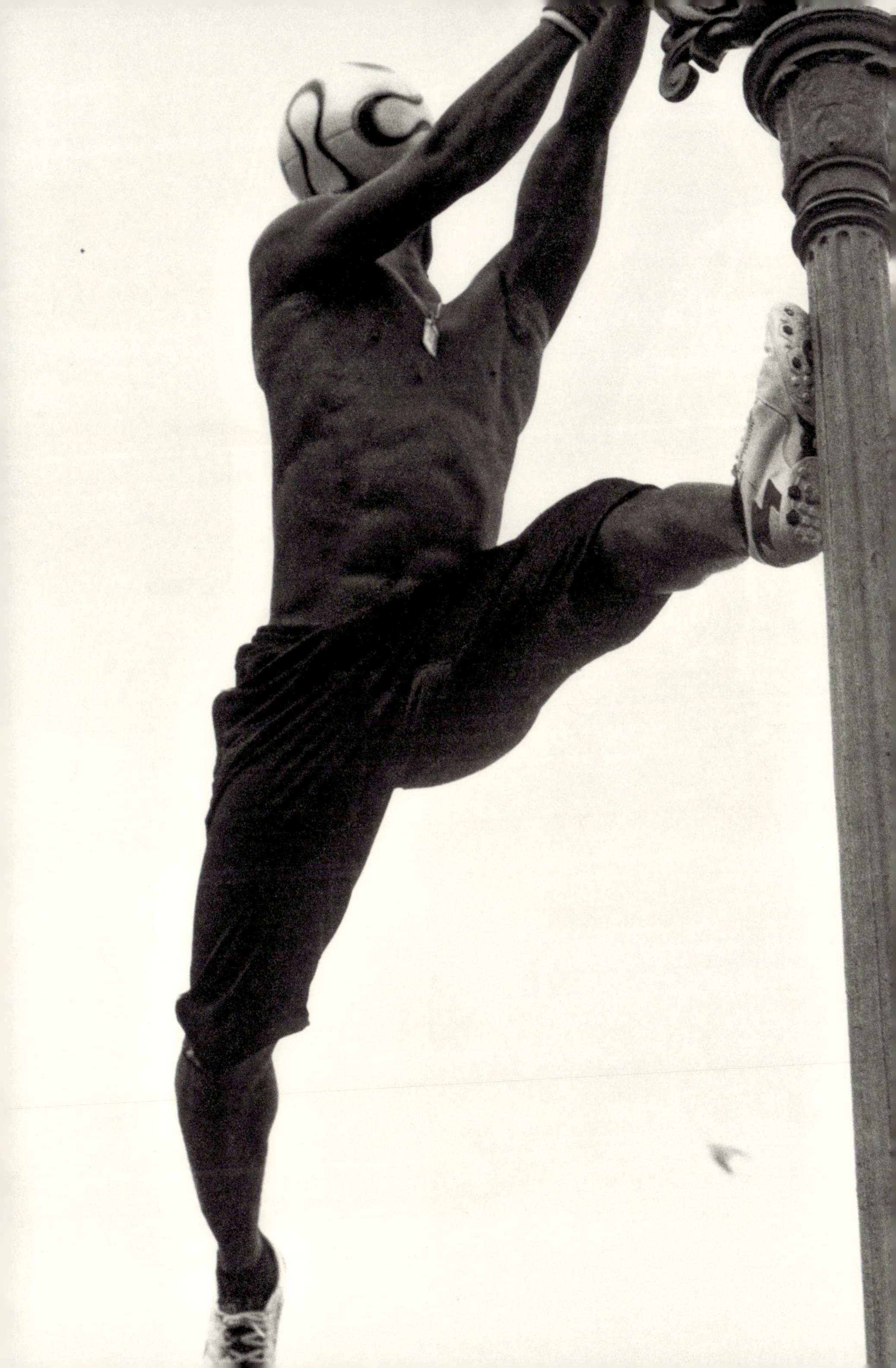

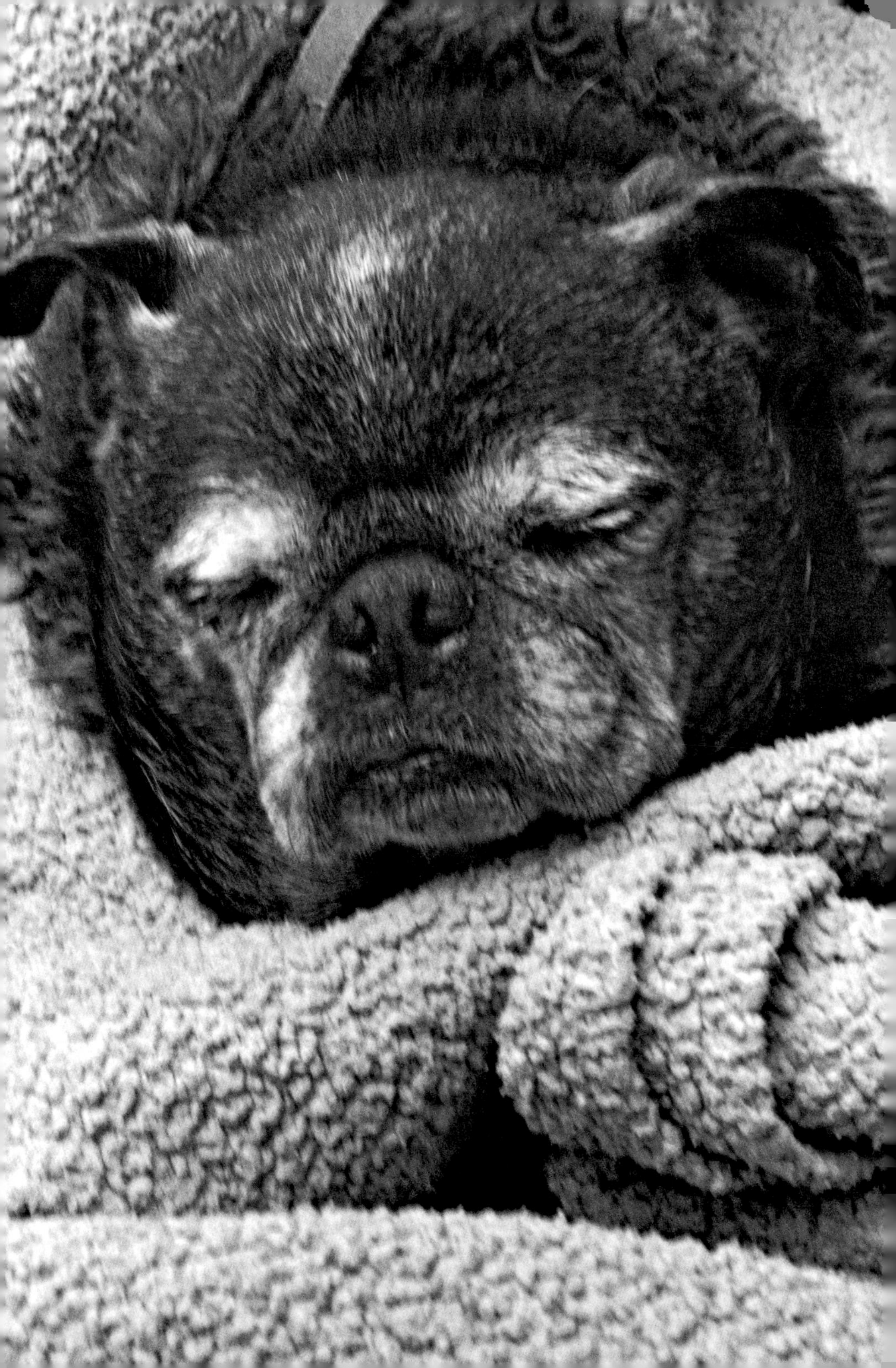

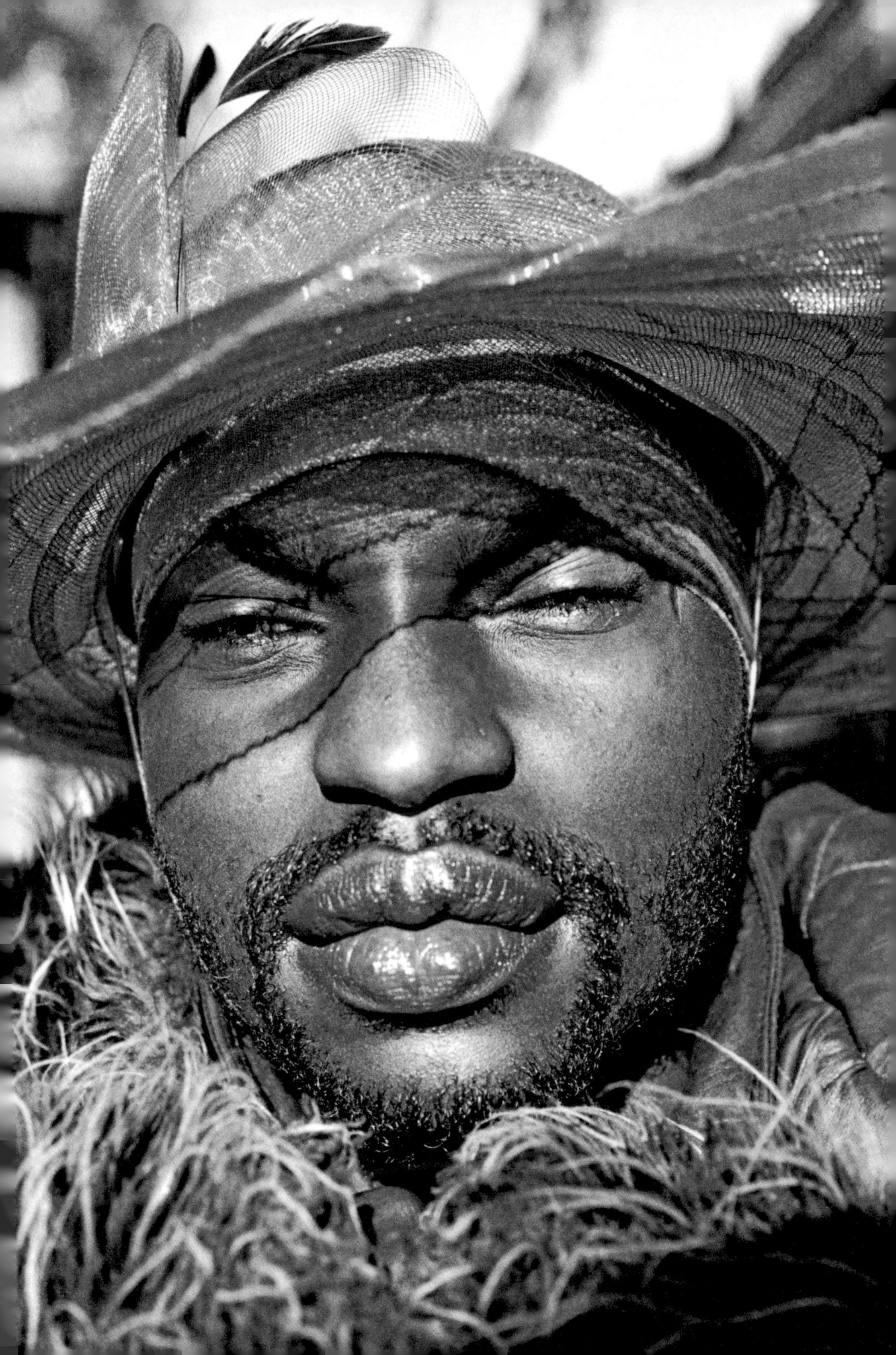

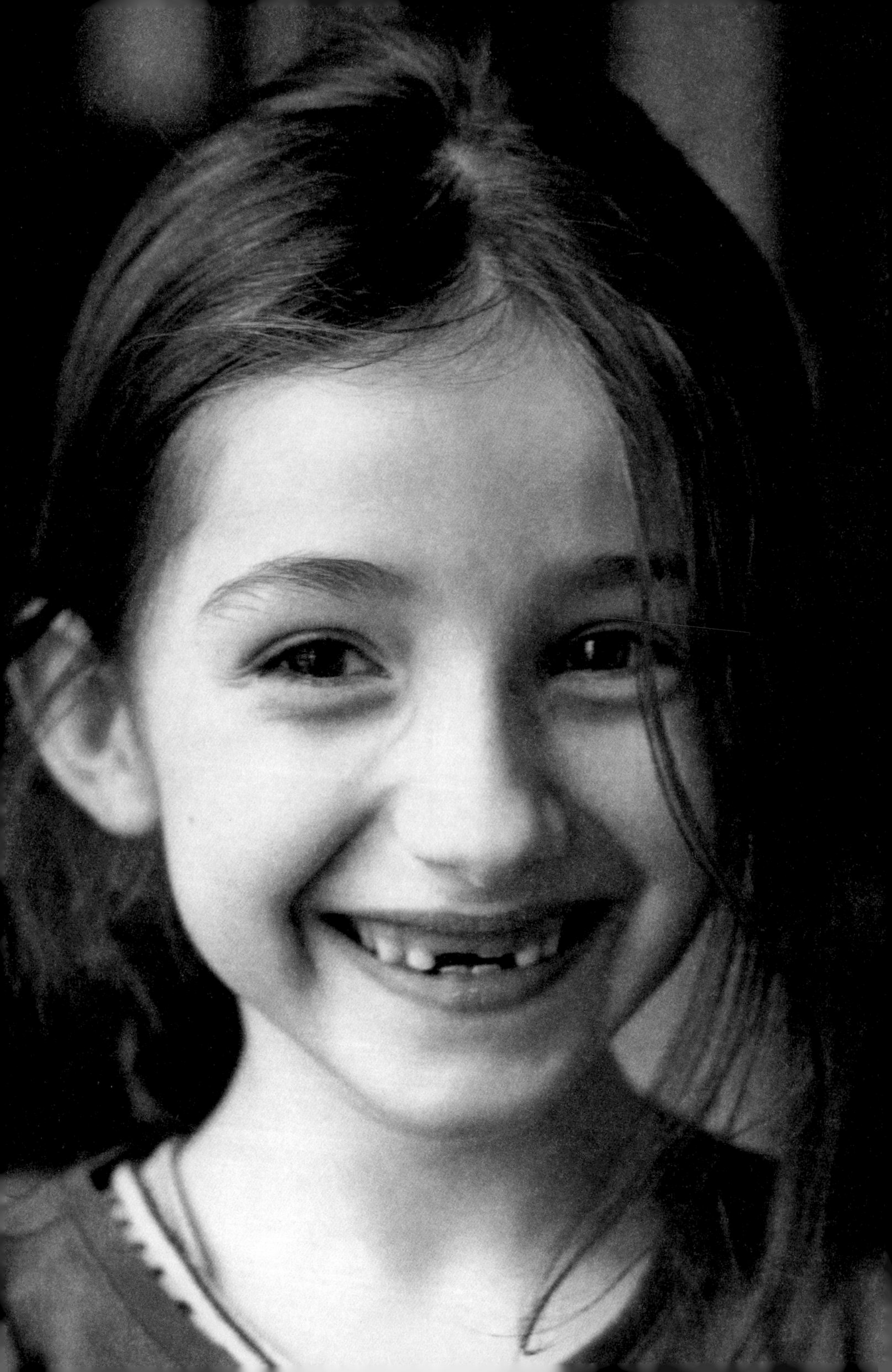

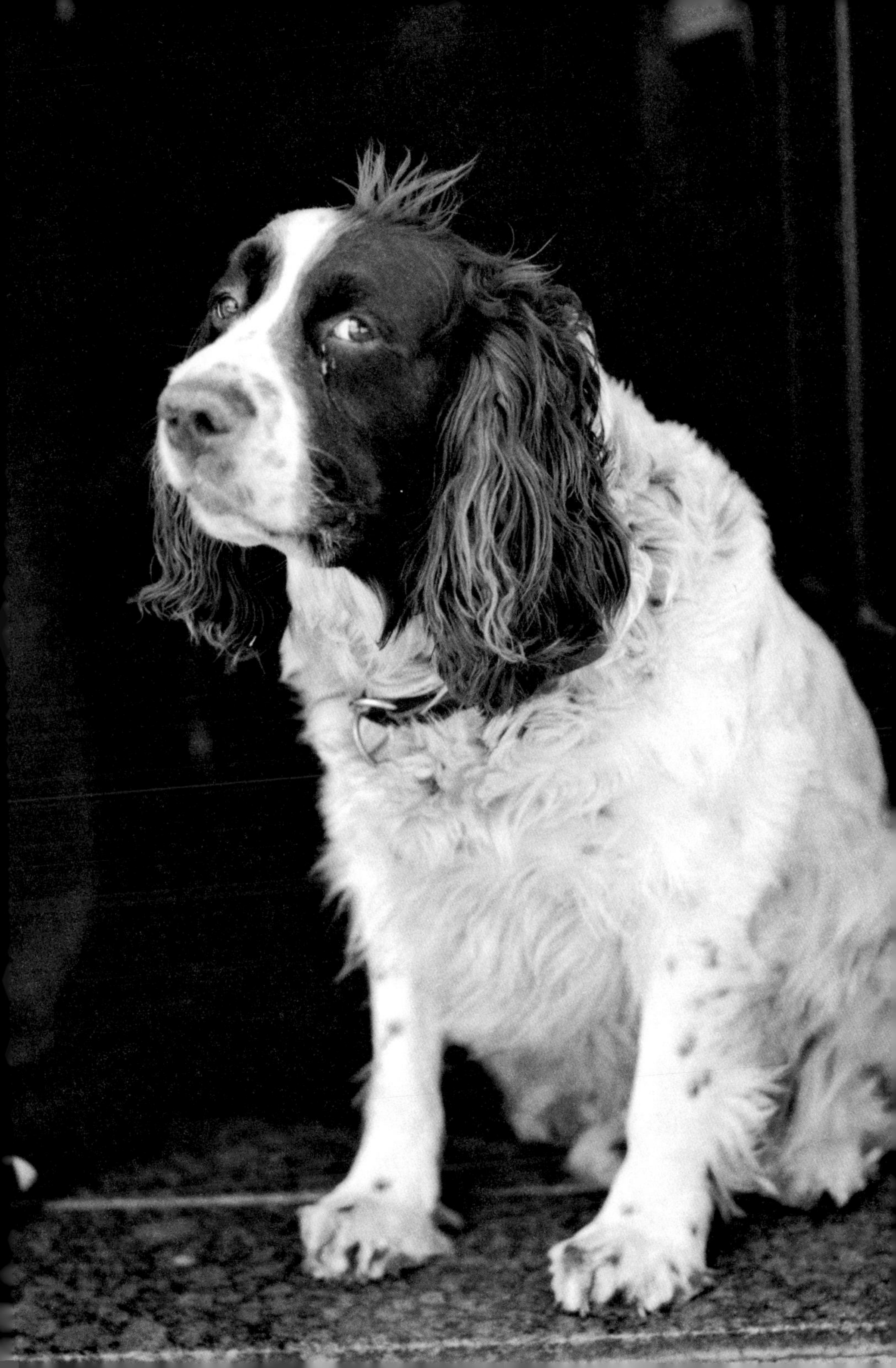

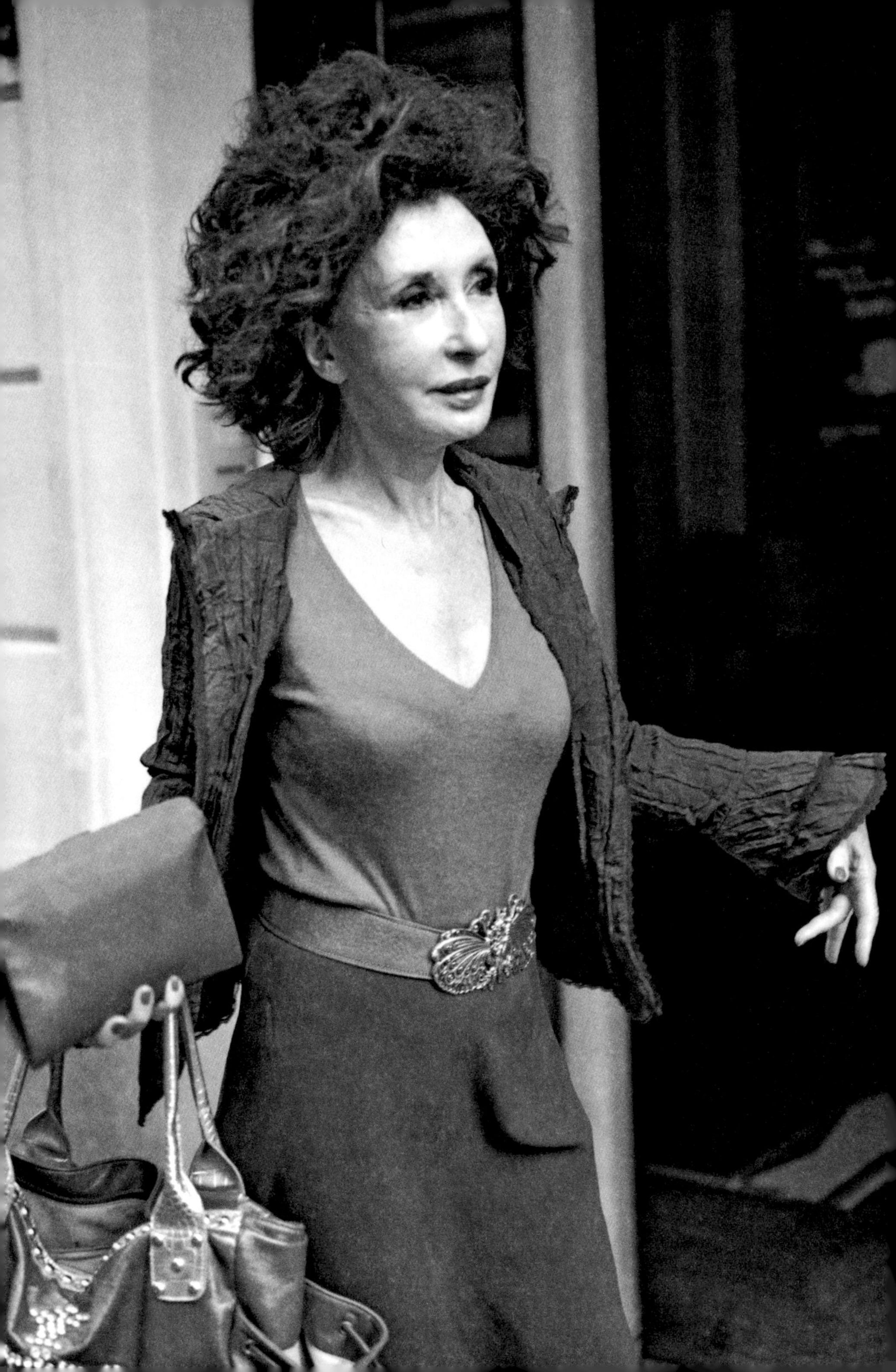

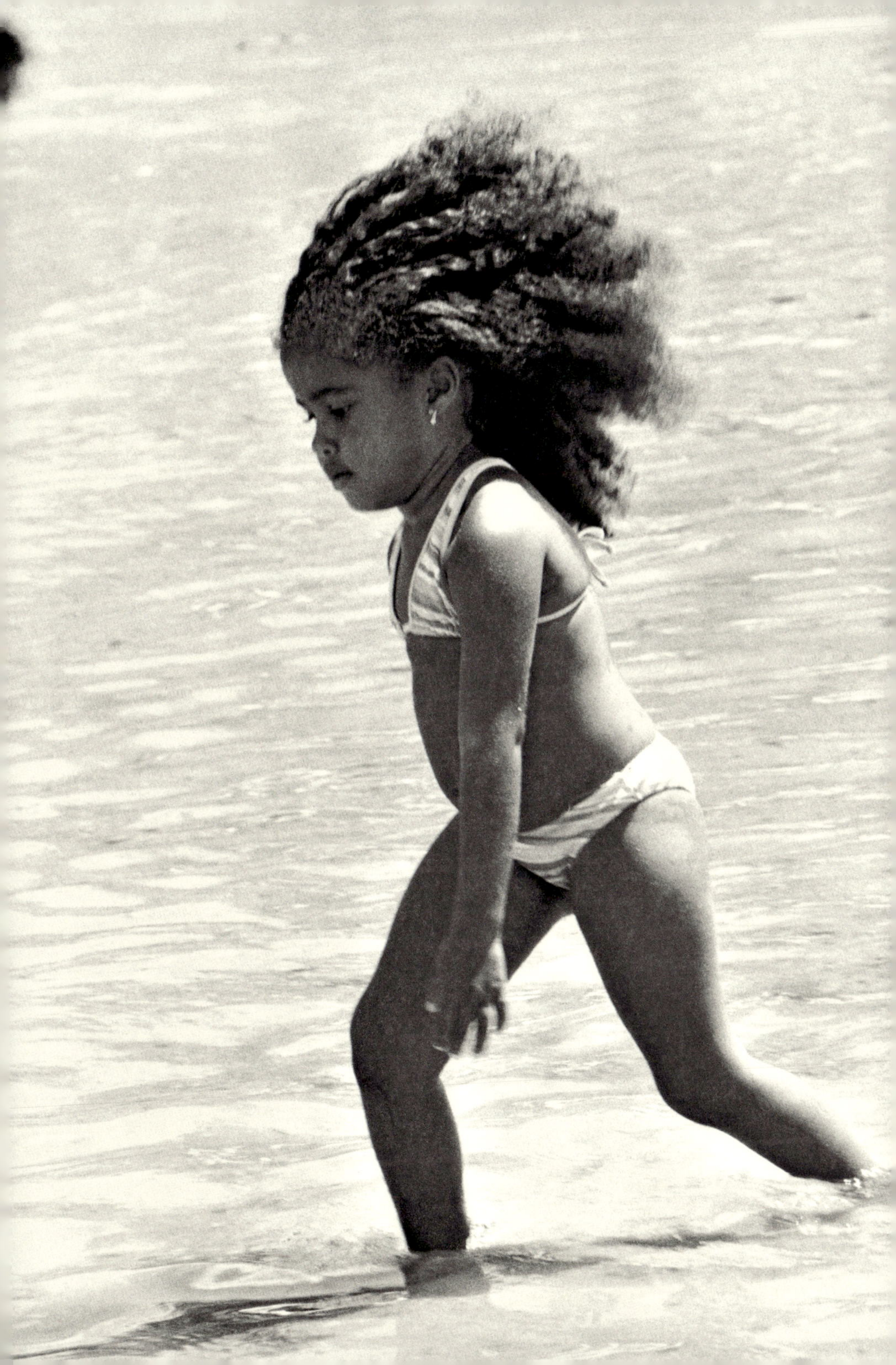

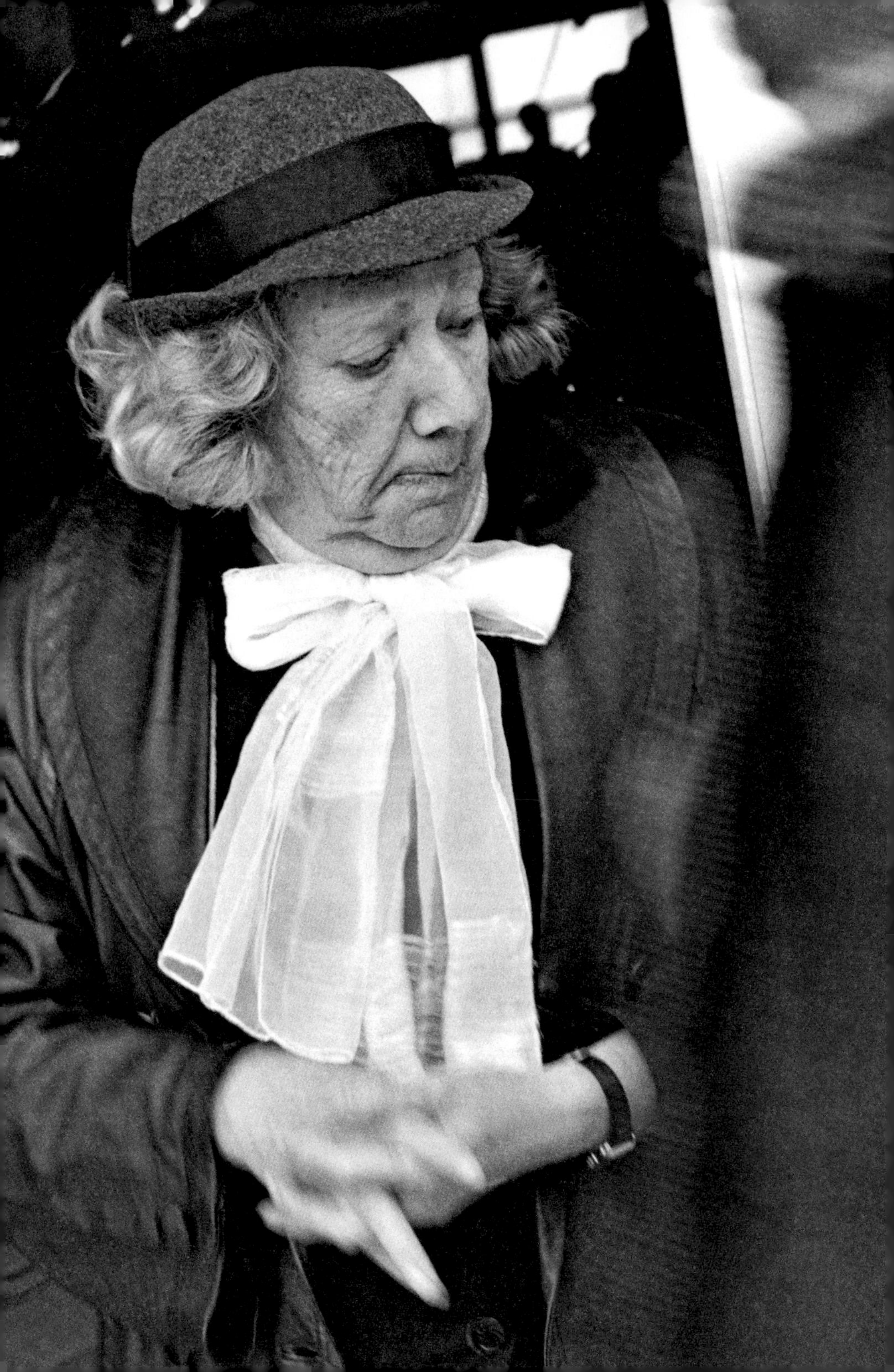

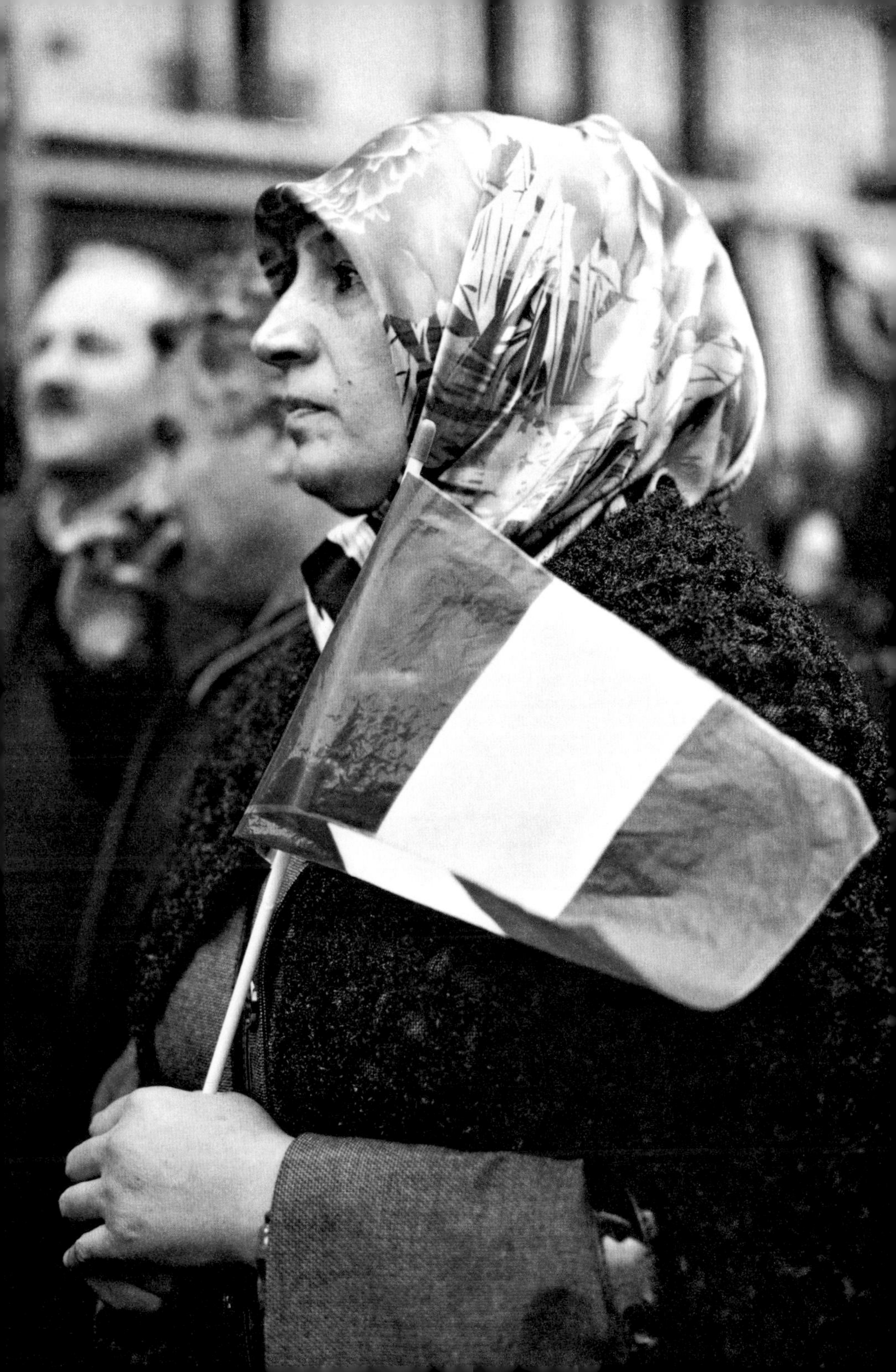

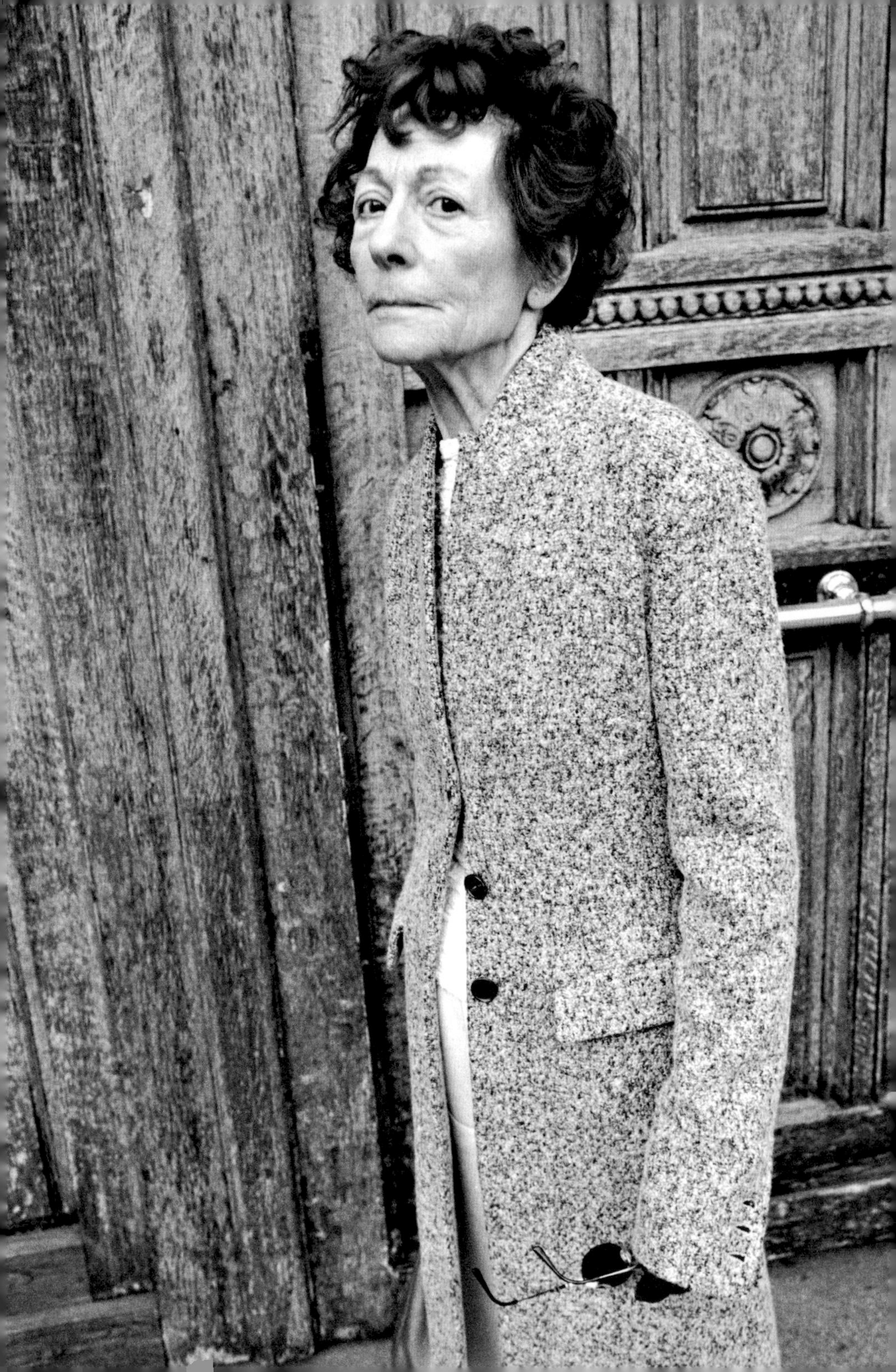

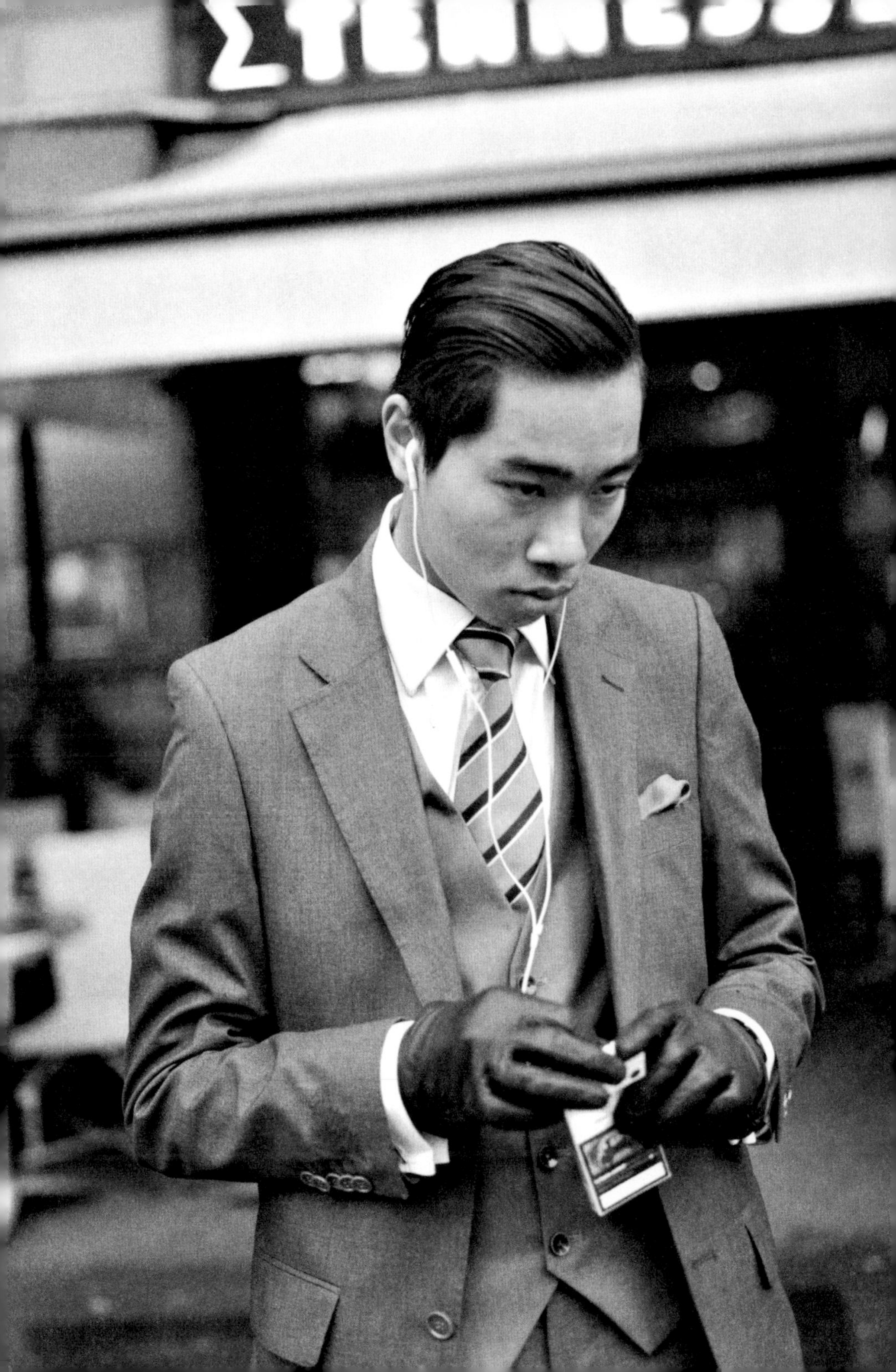
ΣΤΕΝΝΕΣΣ

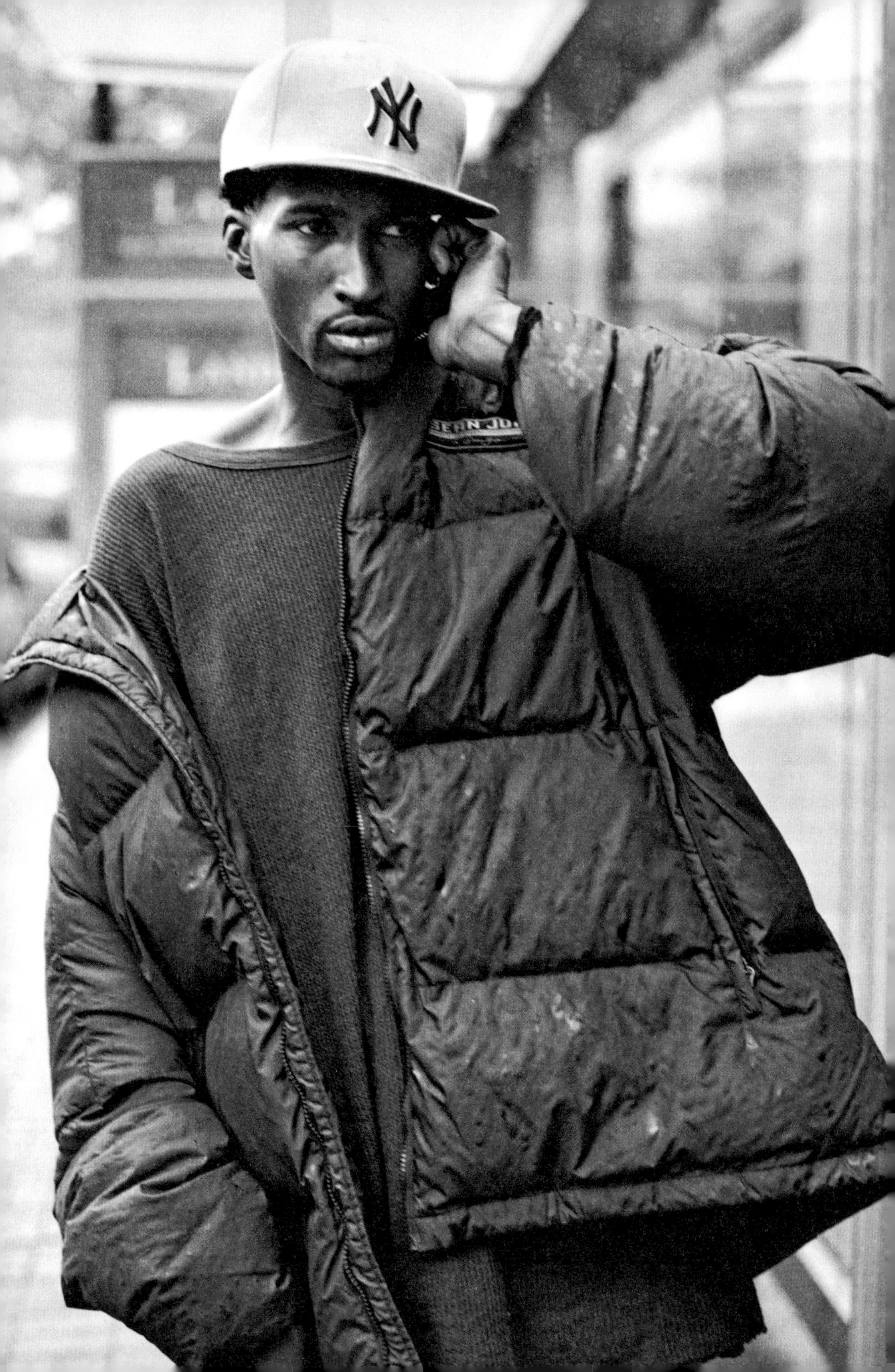

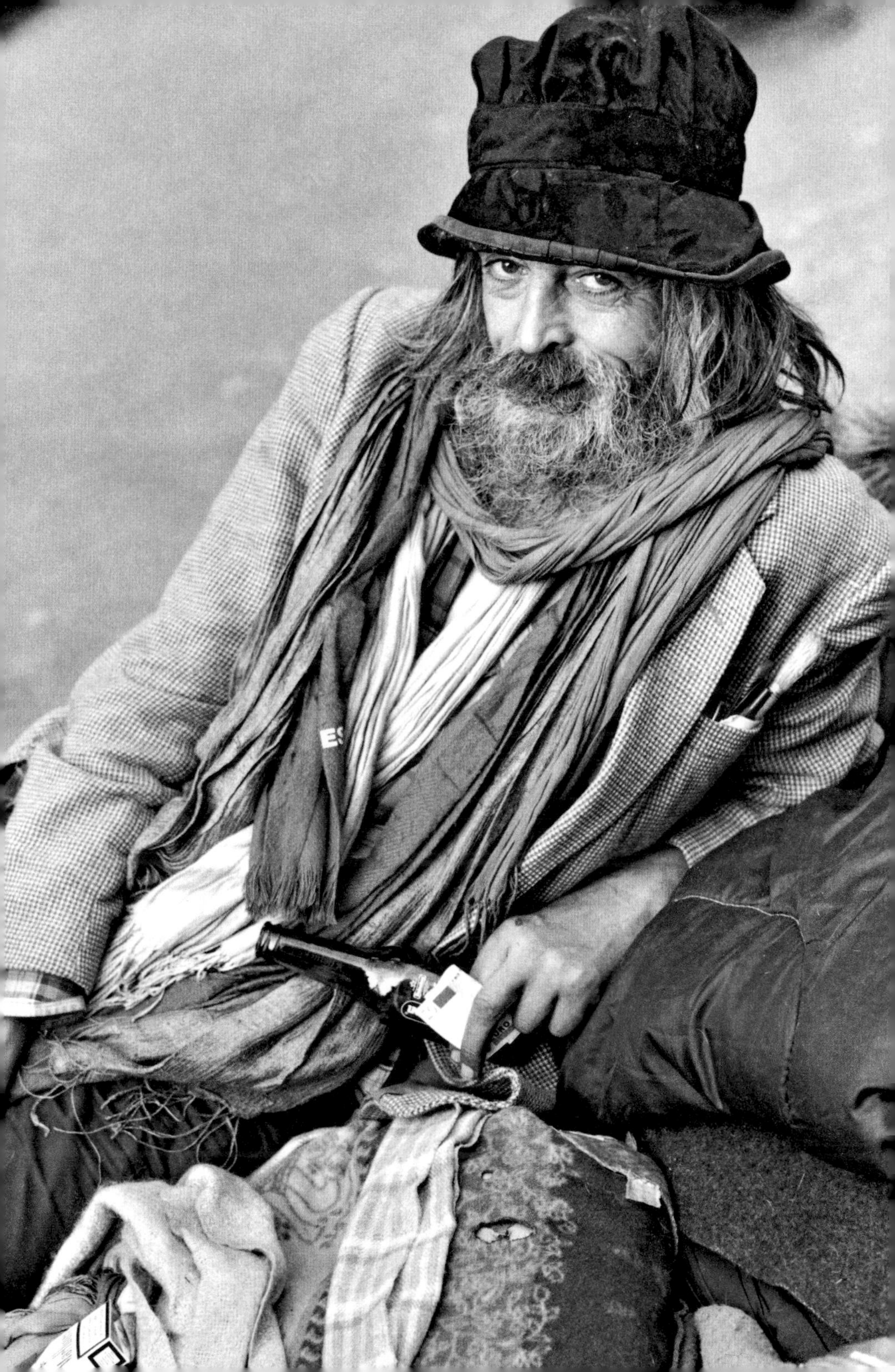

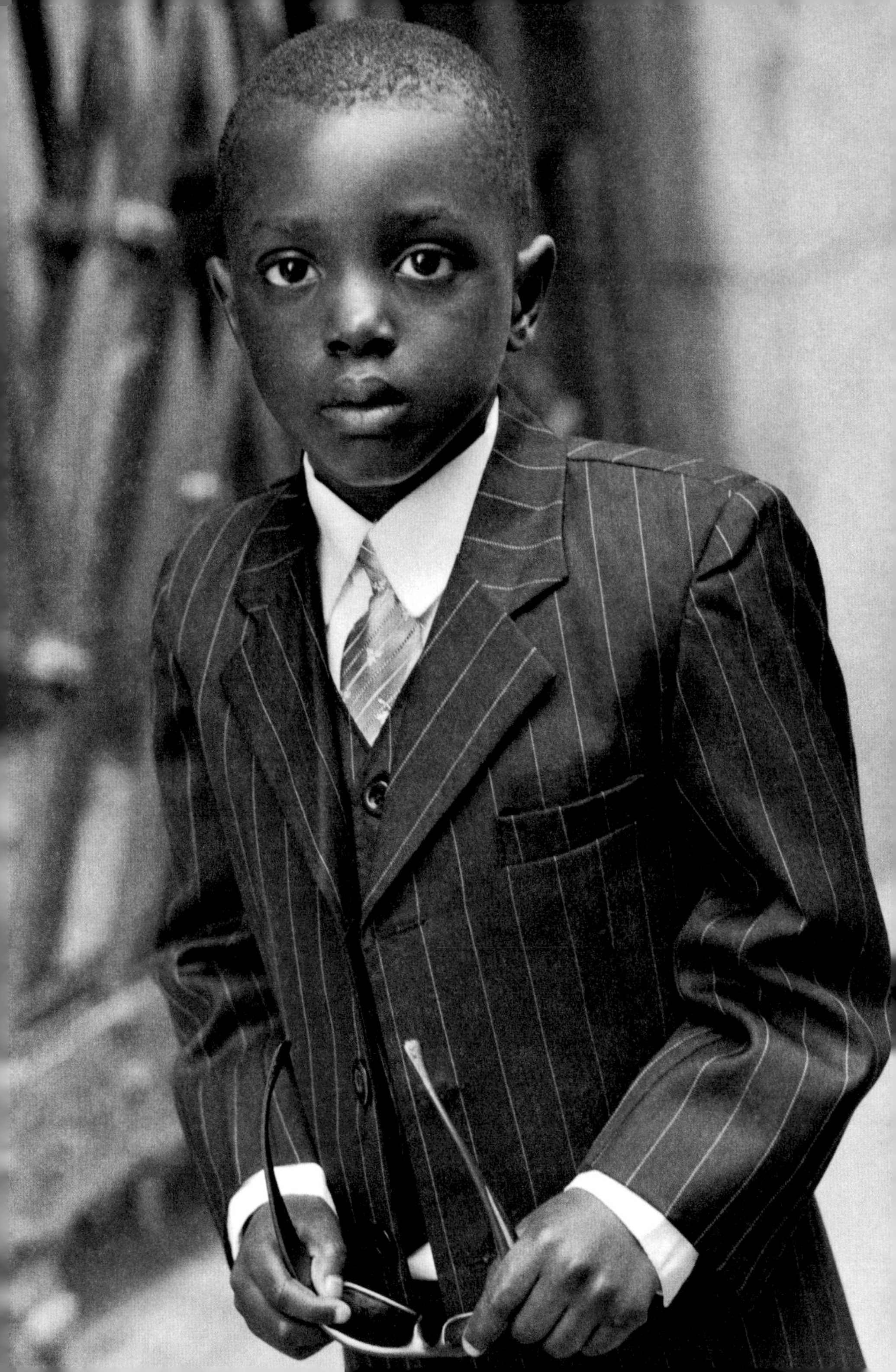

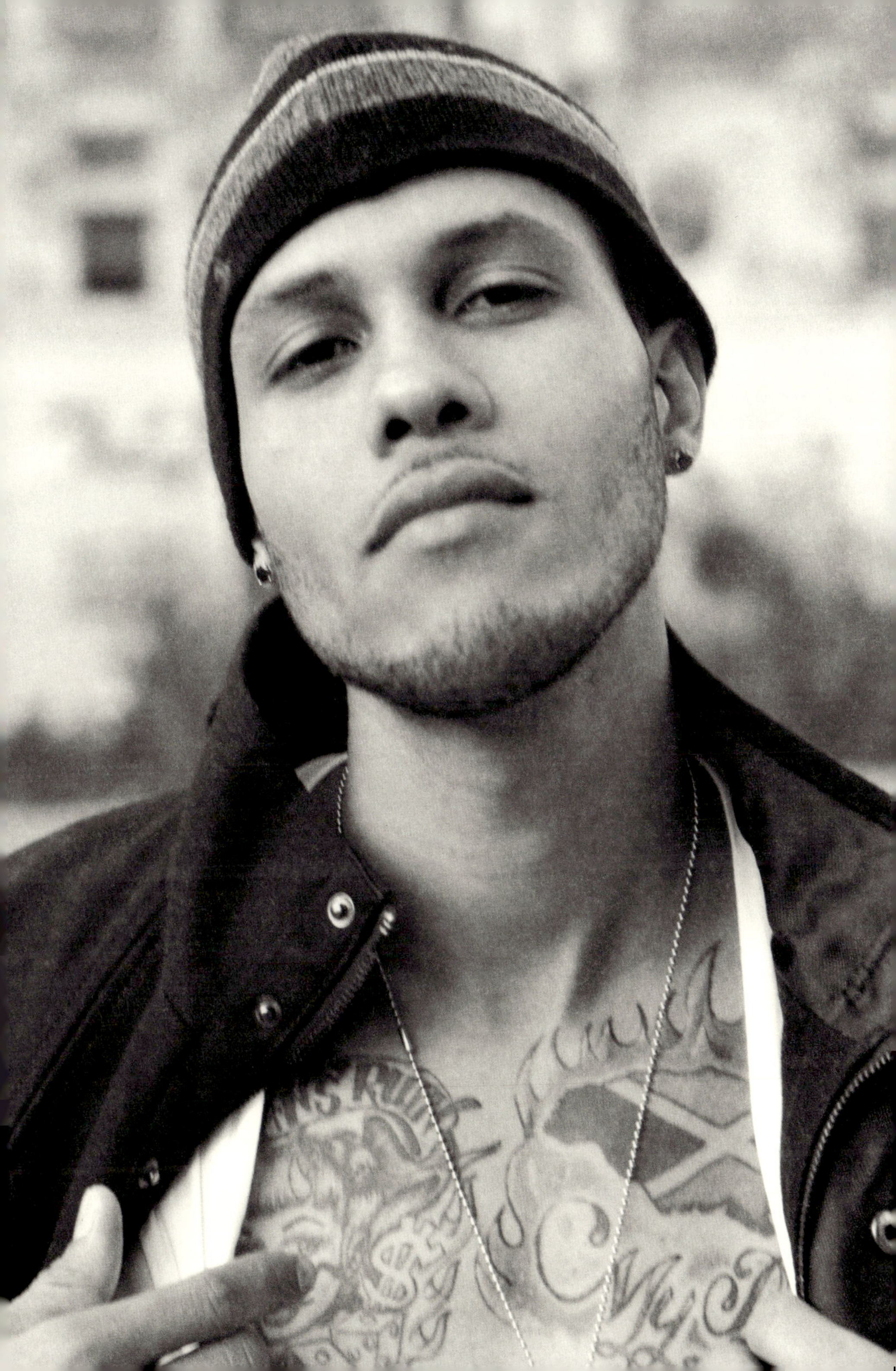

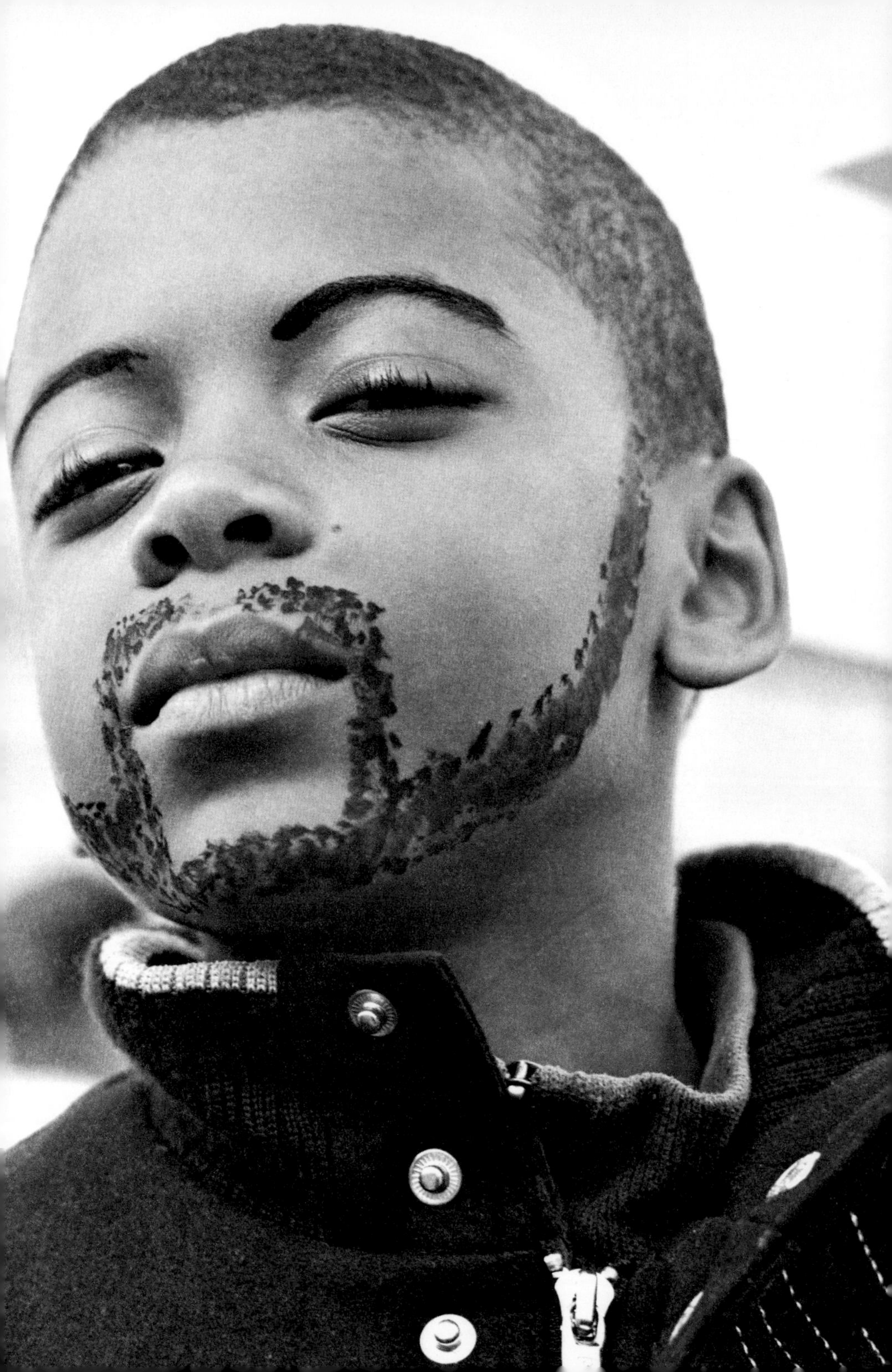

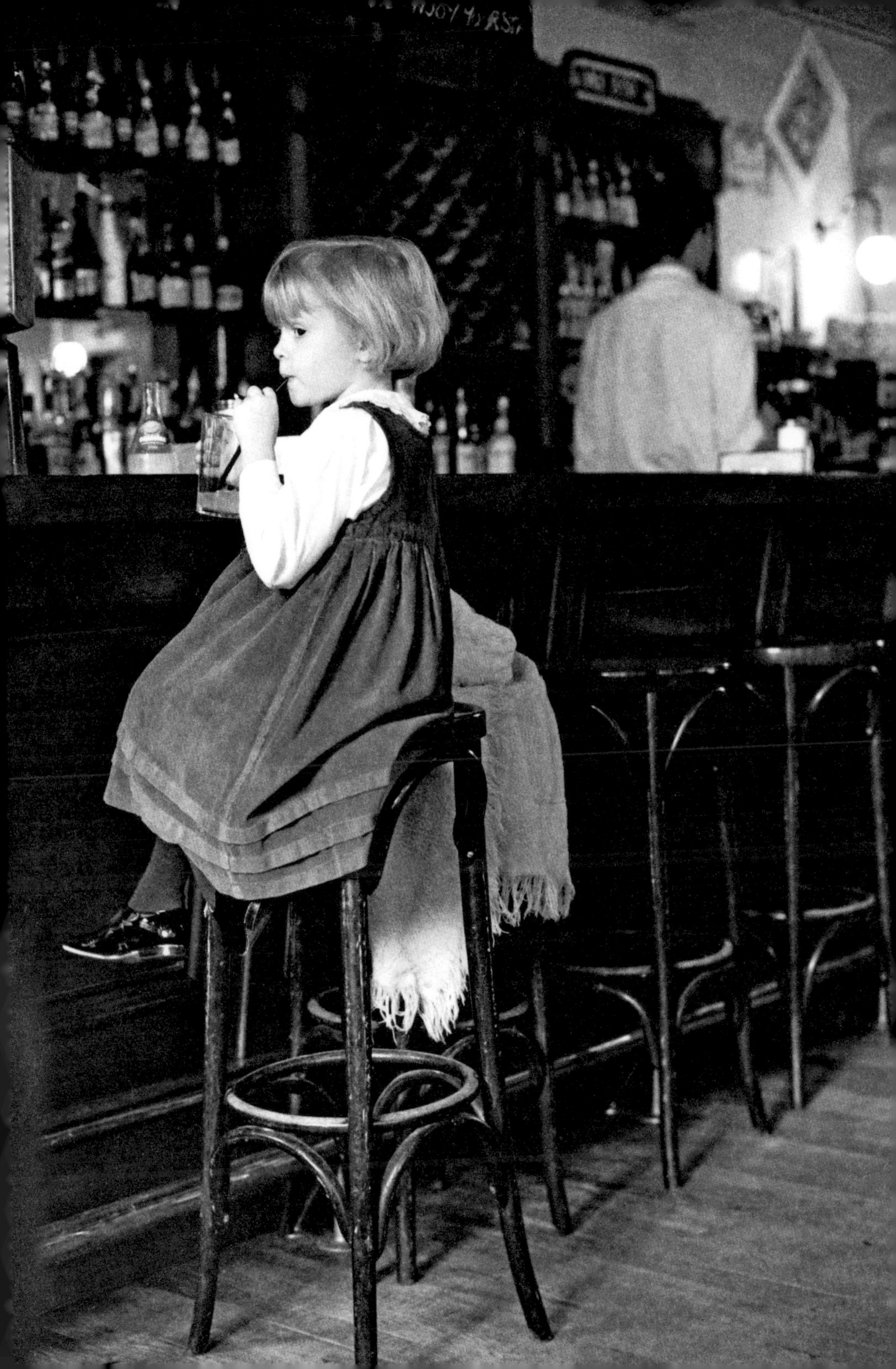

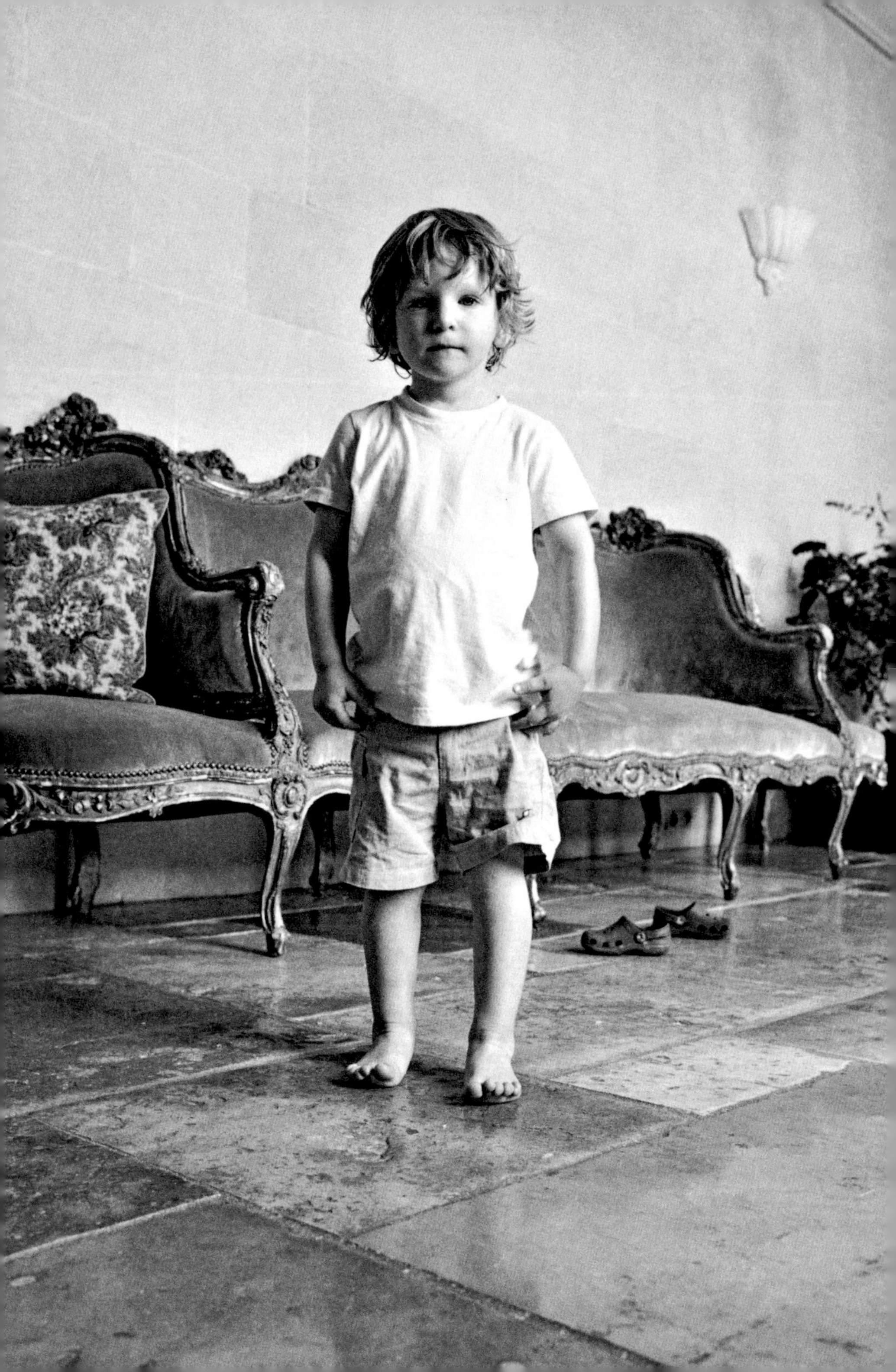

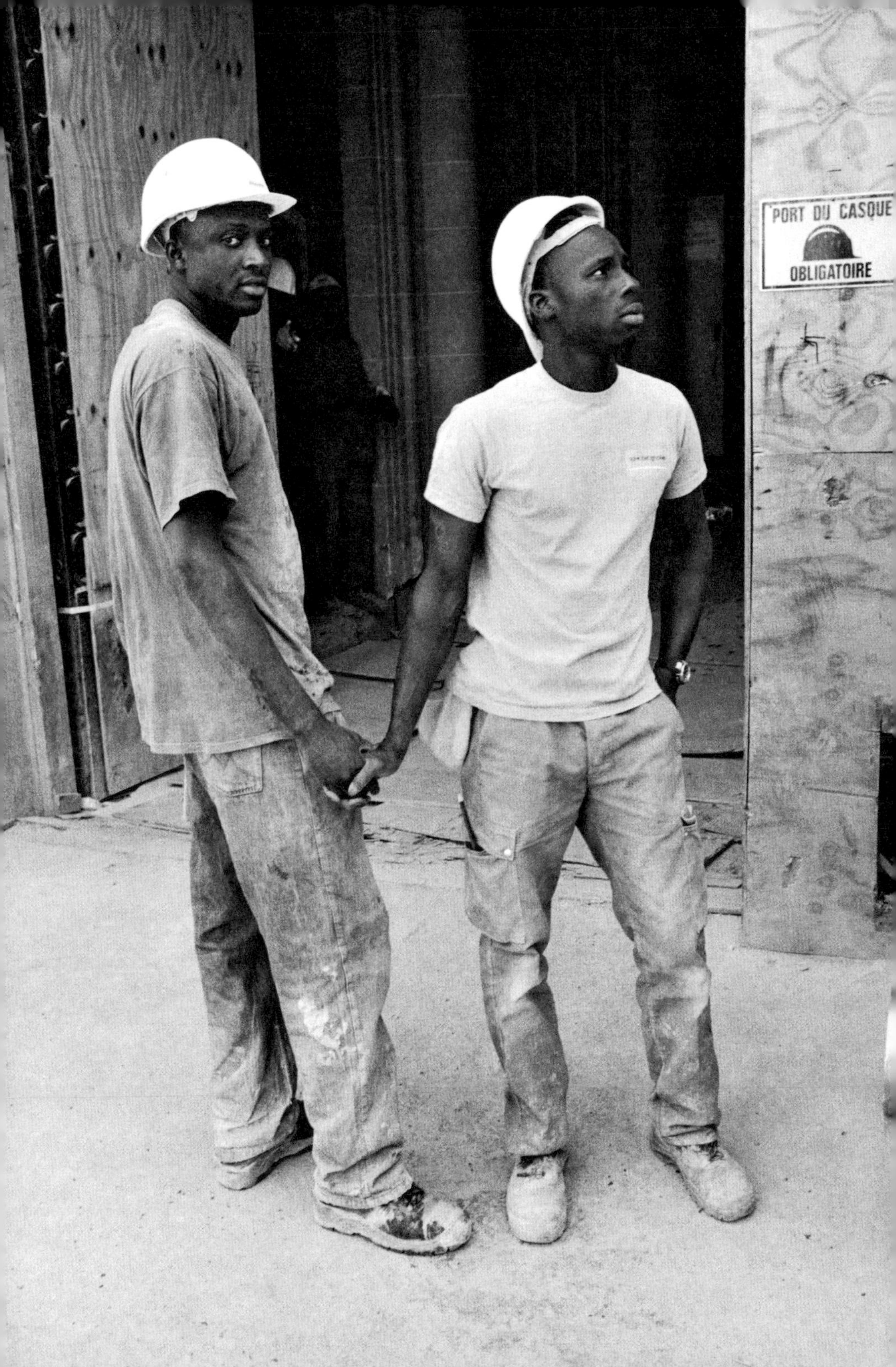
PORT DU CASQUE
OBLIGATOIRE

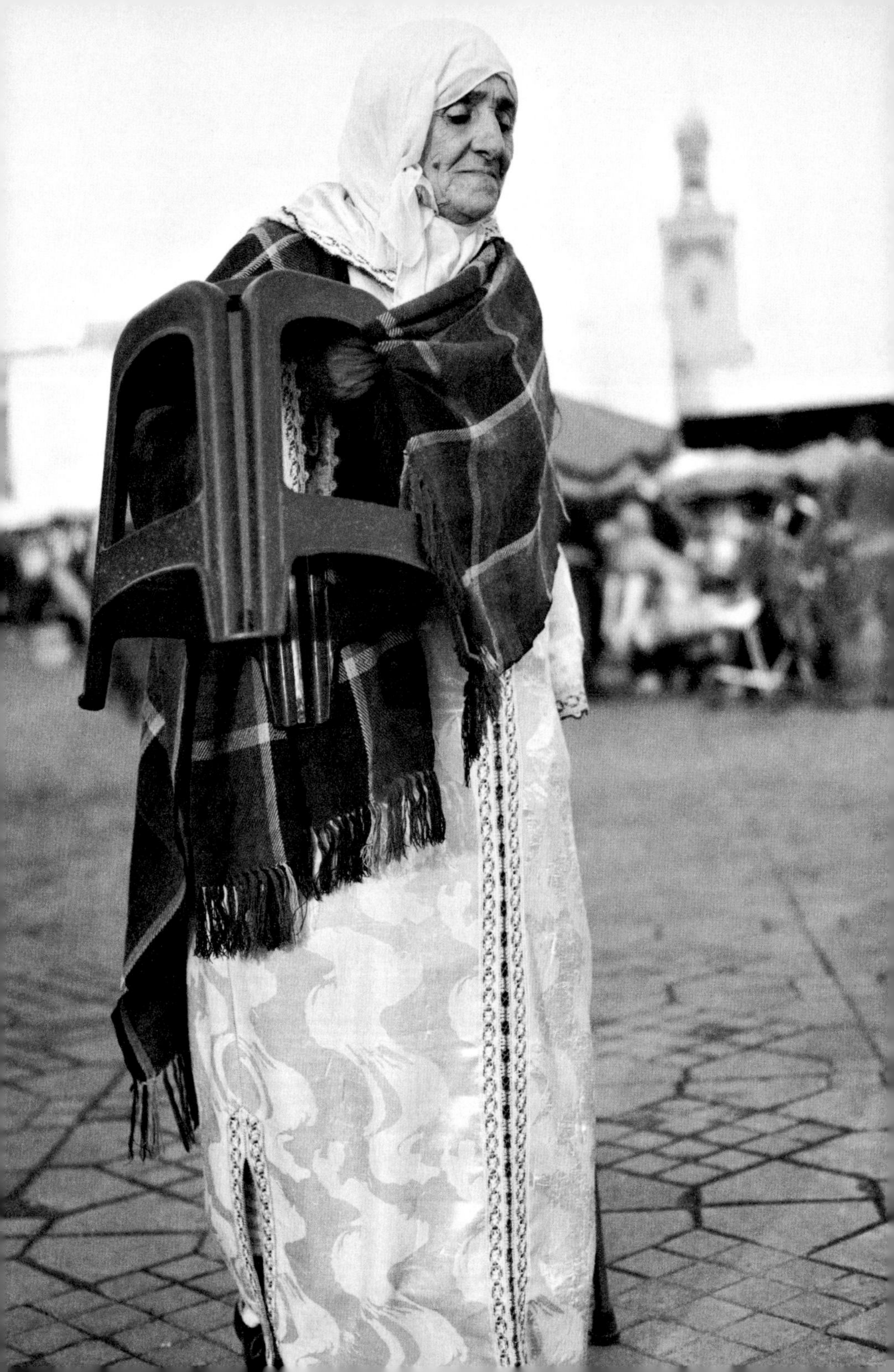

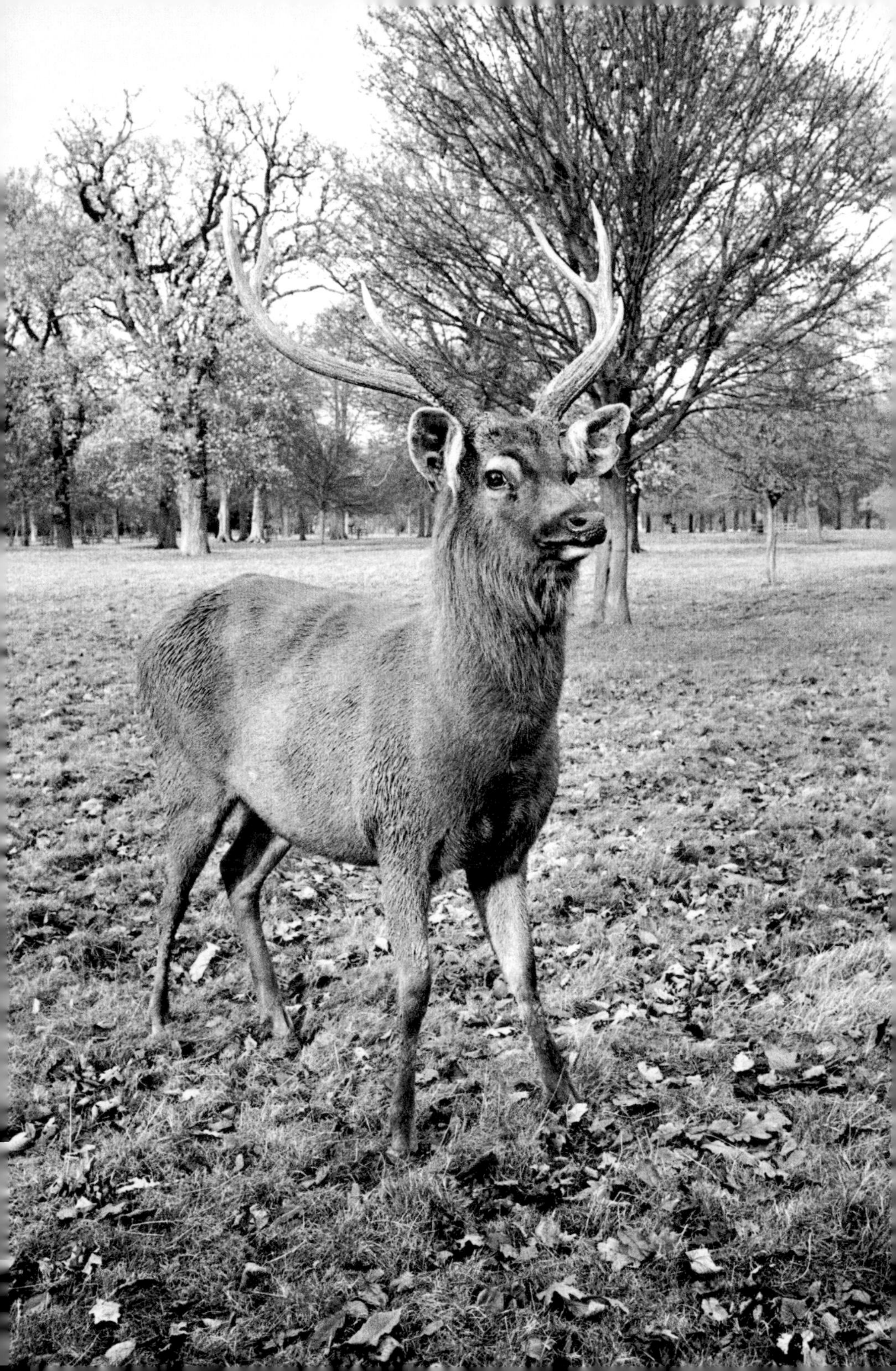

for Jan Hoet,

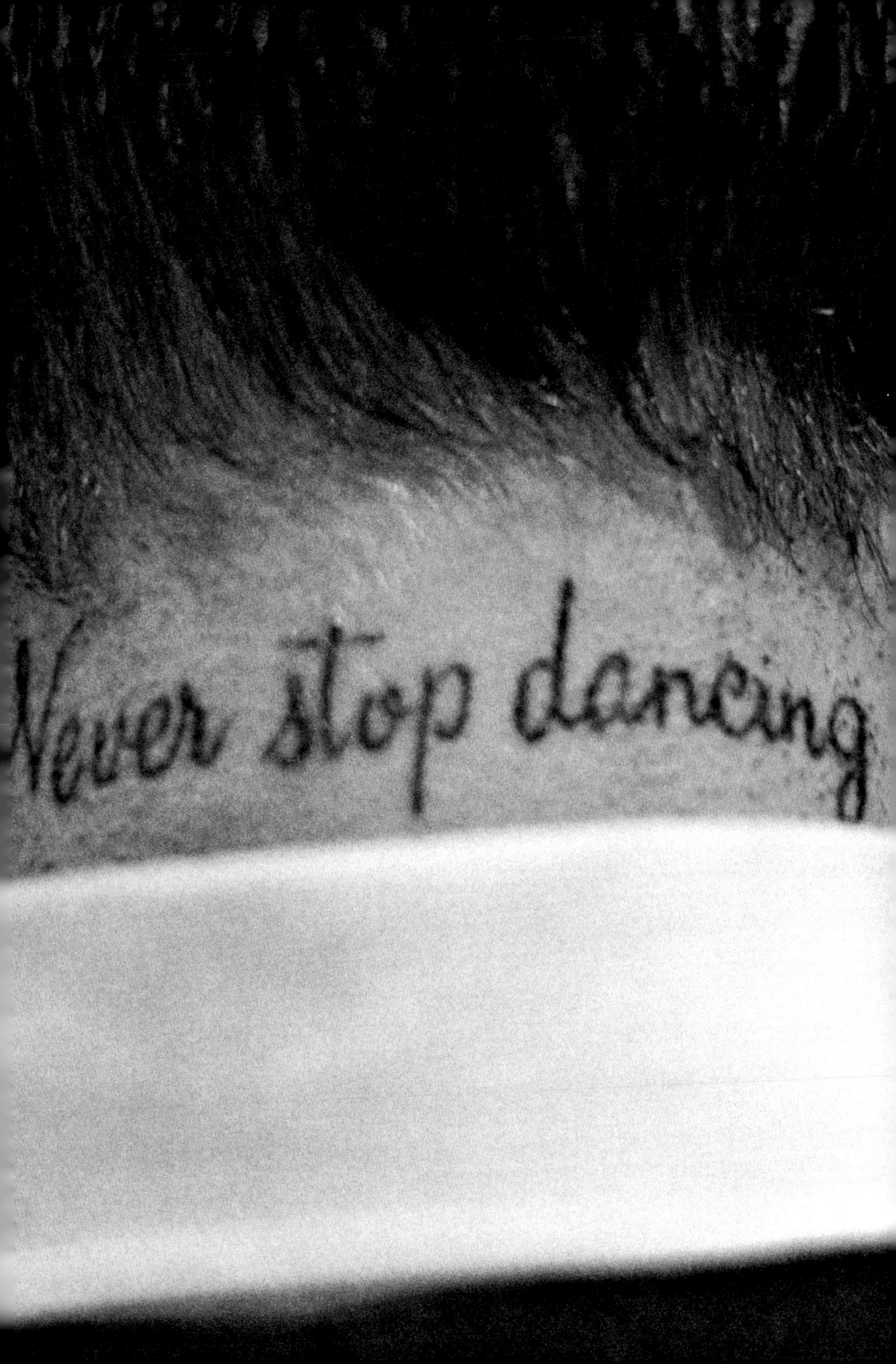

Never stop dancing

Book design by Martin d'Orgeval
and by Gerhard Steidl

published by STEIDL
2015

ISBN 978-3-86930-577-6

Steidl. de